A

LITTLE HOUSE
TRAVELER

Laura and Almanzo shortly after their marriage in De Smet, Dakota Territory.

A
LITTLE HOUSE
TRAVELER

Writings from
Laura Ingalls Wilder's
Journeys Across
America

by

Laura Ingalls Wilder

Collins
An Imprint of HarperCollinsPublishers

Collins is an imprint of HarperCollins Publishers.

A Little House Traveler
Copyright © 2006 by Little House Heritage Trust

On the Way Home: The Diary of a Trip from South Dakota
to Mansfield, Missouri, in 1894
Copyright © 1962, 1990 by Little House Heritage Trust

West from Home: Letters of Laura Ingalls Wilder, San Francisco, 1915
Copyright © 1974 by Little House Heritage Trust

The Road Back: Laura Ingalls Wilder's Record of the Journey
Back to De Smet, South Dakota, 1931
Copyright © 2006 by Little House Heritage Trust

Library of Congress Cataloging-in-Publication Data
Wilder, Laura Ingalls, 1867–1957.
A Little house traveler / by Laura Ingalls Wilder
    p. cm.
  ISBN 978-0-06-072492-4
  [1. Wilder, Laura Ingalls, 1867–1957—Correspondence. 2. Wilder, Laura Ingalls,
1867–1957—Travel—United States. 3. Authors, American—20th century—
Correspondence. 4. United States—Description and travel.] I. Title.
PS3545.I342 Z48 2006
[813'.52 22]-dc22   2005014975
                                                                                           CIP
                                                                                           AC

13 14 15   CG/OPM   10 9 8 7 6 5 4 3
❖
First paperback edition, 2011

CONTENTS

A
LITTLE HOUSE
TRAVELER

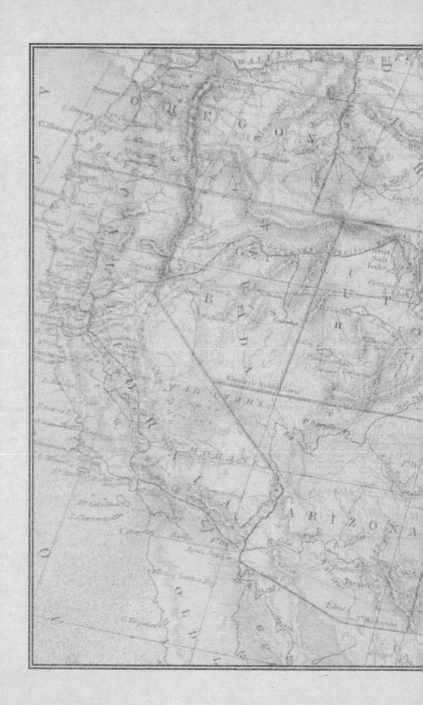

Part One

ON THE WAY HOME

The Diary of a Trip from South Dakota to Mansfield, Missouri, in 1894

With a Setting by Rose Wilder Lane

I was 2 years 4 months old when this picture was taken in April 1889. I remember the picture-taking well, was impressed by the photographer's stupid pretense that there was a little bird in the camera. The photographer also kept putting my right hand on top of the left, and I kept changing them back because I wanted my carnelian ring to show. And in the end I won out.   *Rose Wilder Lane*

One

For seven years there had been too little rain. The prairies were dust. Day after day, summer after summer, the scorching winds blew the dust and the sun was brassy in a yellow sky. Crop after crop failed. Again and again the barren land had to be mortgaged, for taxes and food and next year's seed. The agony of hope ended when there was no harvest and no more credit, no money to pay interest and taxes; the banker took the land. Then the bank failed.

In the seventh year a mysterious catastrophe occurred worldwide—all banks failed. From coast to coast the factories shut down, and business ceased. This was a Panic.

It was not a depression. The year was 1893, when no one had heard of depressions. Everyone knew about Panics; there had been Panics in 1797, 1820, 1835, 1857, 1873. A Panic was nothing new to Grandpa, he had seen them before; this one was no worse than usual, he said, and nothing like as bad as the wartime. Now we were all safe in our beds, nobody was rampaging but Coxey's armies.*

All the way from California Coxey's Armies of Unemployed were seizing the railroad trains, jam-packing the cars and running them full speed, open throttle, hell-for-leather toward Washington. They came roaring into the towns, yelling "Justice for the Working Man!" and stopped and swarmed out, demanding plenty to eat and three days' rations to take with them, or they'd burn the town. People gave them everything to get rid of them. In all the cities Federal troops were guarding the Government's buildings.

I was seven years old and in the Second Reader at school but I had read the Third Reader and the Fourth, and *Robinson Crusoe* and *Gulliver's Travels*. The *Chicago Inter-Ocean* came every

---

*A group of unemployed workers who organized a march on Washington, D.C., to lobby for funds to create jobs.

week and after the grown-ups had read it, I did. I did not understand all of it, but I read it.

It said that east of the Miss-issippi there were no trains on the railroad tracks. The dispatchers had dispatched every train to the faraway East to keep them safe from Coxey's Armies. So now the Armies were disbanded and walking on foot toward Washington, robbing and raiding and stealing and begging for food as they went.

For a long time I had been living with Grandpa and Grandma and the aunts in De Smet because nobody knew what would become of my father and mother. Only God knew. They had diff-theer-eeah; a hard word and dreadful. I did not know what it was exactly, only that it was big and black and it meant that I might never see my father and mother again.

Then my father, man-like, would not listen to reason and stay in bed. Grandma almost scolded about that, to the aunts. Bound and determined to get out and take care of the stock, he was. And for working too hard too soon, he was "stricken." Now he would be bed-ridden all his days, and what would Laura do, my family wondered. With me on her hands, besides.

But when I saw my father again he was walking, slowly. He limped through the rest of his ninety years and was never as strong as he had been, but he was walking.

We lived then in our own house in De Smet, away from Main Street, where only a footpath went through the short brown grasses. It was a big rented house and empty. Upstairs and down it was dark and full of stealthy little sounds at night, but then the lamp was lit in the kitchen, where we lived. Our cookstove and table and chairs were there; the bed was in an empty room and at bedtime my trundle bed was brought into the warmth from the cookstove. We were camping, my mother said; wasn't it fun? I knew she wanted me to say yes, so I did. To me, everything was simply what it was.

I was going to school while my father and mother worked. Reading, writing, spelling, arithmetic, penmanship filled days almost unbearably happy with achievements satisfying Miss Barrows's strict standards. "Procrastination is the thief of time," I wrote twenty times in my penmanship book, without error or blot; and "Evil communications corrupt good manners," and "Sweet are the uses of adversity," every t and d exactly twice as tall as a vowel and every l exactly three times as tall; every t crossed; every i dotted.

WILLIAM ANDERSON

Rose (4th from left) in her church's "children's exercises" just before leaving De Smet in 1894.

All the way home down the long board walk in late afternoons we diligent scholars warmly remembered our adored Miss Barrows's grave, "Well done," and often we sang a rollicking song. It was the song of those days, heard more often than Ta-ra-ra boom-de-ay. My aunt Grace, a jolly big girl, often sang it, sometimes my mother did, and nearly all the time you could hear some man or boy whistling it.

BOTH: LAURA INGALLS WILDER HOME ASSOCIATION

Laura (top) and Almanzo (bottom) at the time of These Happy Golden Years.

On the Way Home

O Dakota land, sweet Dakota land,
As on thy burning soil I stand
And look away across the plains
I wonder why it never rains,
Till Gabriel blows his trumpet sound
And says the rain has gone around.
We don't live here, we only stay
'Cause we're too poor to get away.

My mother did not have to go out to work; she was married, my father was the provider. He got a day's work here and there; he could drive a team, he could carpenter, or paint, or spell a storekeeper at dinner-time, and once he was on a jury, downtown. My mother and I slept at Grandma's then, every night; the jury was kept under lock and key and my father could not come home. But he got his keep and two dollars every day for five straight weeks and he brought back all that money.

My mother worked to save. She sewed at the dressmaker's from six o'clock to six o'clock every day but Sunday and then came home to get supper. I had peeled the potatoes thin and set the table. I was not allowed to touch the stove. One day my mother made sixty good firm buttonholes in one hour, sixty minutes; nobody else could work so well, so fast. And every day, six days a week, she earned a dollar.

We were saving to go to The Land of the Big Red Apple. Someone named Mr. Sherwin had gone there and seen it, so the pictures that he sent back were true; pictures of huge red apples and of rows of much smaller trees, and of buildings confusingly named Mansfield. They were not a man's field, and the print under them said they were The Gem City of the Ozarks.

Around and under these pictures on beautifully shiny paper I read that The Gem City of the Ozarks was in The Land of the Big Red Apple in Missouri. Now I knew three Miss States: Mississippi, Miss-consin, and Miss-ouri. Paul said, scornfully, that it wasn't Miss-consin, it was *Wis*-consin, but Wis didn't make sense to me.

Paul and George Cooley were coming with us to The Land of the Big Red Apple. Paul was oldest, George was next, I was the youngest but they had to let me boss them around because I was a girl. We had always known each other. Their father had two big teams and two big covered wagons, and Paul would be allowed to drive one of them; he said his father said he could. I did not want to believe this but I knew that Paul would never lie.

He was a big boy, too, going on ten years old.

My mother had saved one hundred dollars to take to The Land of the Big Red Apple. All those dollars were one piece of paper, named "a hundred dollar bill." She hid it in her writing desk, a fascinating wooden box which my father had made and polished so shiny-smooth that stroking it was rapture. It opened on little brass hinges to lie spread flat and be a slanting green felt surface to write on. At the top was a darling wooden tray to hold my mother's pearl-handled pen, and beside this was an inkwell. And the green felt was on a lid that lifted up on tinier hinges to reveal the place for writing paper, underneath it. I was allowed to see and touch the desk only when my mother opened it.

The hundred dollar bill was a secret. My mother locked it in the desk. Mr. and Mrs. Cooley knew, perhaps Paul and George did, but we did not talk about it. I must never, never, speak one word about that hundred dollar bill, not to anyone. Never, no matter what happened.

In the shade of the big empty house my father painted our covered wagon. It was really better than a covered wagon; it had been a two-seated hack though now it had only the front seat. My father painted it shiny black. He made a flat top for

A sewing box made of cigar boxes by Almanzo for a first anniversary gift to Laura. It came with us in the hack to Mansfield. R.W.L.

it, of black oilcloth, and put straight curtains of the black oilcloth on both sides and the back. Each curtain would roll up when he pulled a rope. Behind the seat he fitted the bedsprings and my mother made up the bed on them. At night she would make my bed on the floor in front of the seat.

She baked two dozen hardtacks for the journey. They were as large as a plate, flat and hard. Being so hard and dry, they would not spoil as bread would. It was a hard tack to gnaw, but it tasted almost like a cracker.

We were going to make haste, driving every day to reach The Land of the Big Red Apple and get settled before winter. We could not stop to look for work, but we would need more food on the way, so my father bought a box of asbestos fire mats to trade, or to sell for ten cents apiece.

Fire mats were a new thing, unheard-of. They looked like round pieces of gray-white pasteboard edged with a narrow strip of tin. Nobody could believe that they would not burn, till my father proved it. He would urge doubters to make a hot fire, hotter and hotter, then he laid one of those mats right into the flames. It would glow red and the watchers would jeer, but that mat came out unharmed. Put one of those fire mats under a pot, my father would say, and the pot could boil bone-dry, not a potato in it would so much as scorch. Every woman alive needed one of those mats.

Everything that we were taking all the way was

packed under the bedsprings first. Next, the things that we would be using: the table and chairs with folding legs and the sheet-iron campstove that my father had made; the hammock that blind Aunt Mary had netted and given to us as a parting present; the writing desk, well wrapped; plates, cups, frying pan, coffee pot, wash basin, water pail, picket ropes and pegs; the hardtack in its box. My father tied down the back curtain. Outside it he fastened the hencoop while the hens fluttered and squawked inside the wire netting. But they would soon be used to traveling.

In the dawn next morning we said goodbye to Grandpa and Grandma, to the aunts Mary and Carrie and Grace, who all stood around to watch us go, though Aunt Mary's beautiful blue eyes could not see us. The mares were hitched to the hack; their colts, Little Pet and Prince, would follow them. The Cooleys' covered wagons had gone ahead, and Paul was driving the second one. I climbed up over our wagon's wheel and onto the seat by myself. My mother sat beside me; beside her my father tightened the lines; everyone said, "Goodbye goodbye!" "Don't forget to write. I won't, I will, you be sure to. Goodbye!" and we drove away.

Laura (top) and Almanzo (bottom) at the time of their trip to Mansfield, Missouri.

Pa and Ma Ingalls' house in De Smet. This picture was sent to us in Mansfield some years after we left Dakota.

R.W.L.

18

Away from Grandma's house with its rag carpets and rocking-chair, the hymn books on the organ, my very own footstool; away from the chalky schoolroom where angelic Miss Barrows taught Kindergarten, Primer, First and Second Readers; away from the summer sidewalks where grasshoppers hopped in the dry grass and the silver-lined poplar leaves rattled overhead; away from the gaunt gray empty house, and from Mrs. Sherwood and her sister who sometimes on sweltering afternoons asked me to fetch ten cents' worth of ice cream from the far-away ice cream parlor, and shared it with me; away from De Smet to The Land of the Big Red Apple.

My mother made daily notes of our journey in a little 5-cent Memorandum book, writing with pencil on both sides of the pages, of course. Nobody then wasted paper. This is her record.

Rose Wilder Lane

Calumet Avenue, De Smet, South Dakota, around 1900.

Two

July 17, 1894

STARTED AT 8:40. Three miles out, Russian thistles. Harvesters in poor wheat. Crossed the line into Miner County at 2 o'clock. Camped by a spring that cannot be pumped, but there is feed for the horses. Grain about 8 inches high, will go about 1½ bushels to the acre. Hot wind.

<hr>

July 18

FARMERS MOWING the grain for hay. At 11:30 we left Howard one mile east. Farm work well along here. Dragging for next year's crop is all done, without troubling to take this year's grain off. Worst crops

21

we have seen yet. No grass. Standing grain 3 inches high, burned brown and dead.

Crossed the Northwestern R.R. tracks at 2:25. Crossed the line into McCook County at 5 o'clock, drove 2½ miles and camped. We had a little dust storm in the afternoon and drew the wagons up close together for we could not see what was coming. The wind changed from a hot south wind to a cold north wind, both *hard*. Though the thermometer stood at 102° in the wagon.

July 19

IT RAINED IN THE NIGHT but did not blow. Nothing in the wagons got wet except one horse blanket. We had fried chicken for breakfast and got a late start at 9:15. Weather is cool and pleasant, wind in the north and dust laid by the rain. Groves are thick and look so nice but farmers are mowing their grain for hay.

We found a good camping place down in a ravine, out of the wind and nearly out of sight. Cooked our supper and ate it. As we were washing the dishes a man came and said if the man that owned the place saw us he would make us trouble, and as he lived just over the hill we thought we would move across the road and be all right there.

So we hitched up and drove across. It was a very nice camping place. In the evening two men came up to talk. The thermometer stood at 92°.

Mrs. Cooley and I went to a house to buy milk. It was swarming with children and pigs; they looked a good deal alike.

~~~

July 20

STARTED AT 7:10. One of the Cooleys' horses cut his leg a little on a barb wire fence.

We left Bridgewater half a mile to the east. Mr. Cooley drove into the town but we went on just south of it with the rest of the teams, and we came to the first piece of oats worth cutting that we have seen since we left De Smet, and still, they are not very good.

We watered the teams at a public well with windmill, by the side of the road. The water is good all through McCook County. Wells are 120 feet deep on the average and nearly every well has a windmill. This is a good county. All through McCook, this year is the first crop failure in 16 years, There are lots of groves of trees, and nice houses, big corncribs, many hogs; but we have not seen many cattle though there is a creamery in

Bridgewater. The people say the corn crop is very poor but it is the best we have ever seen at this time of year.

Crossed the line into Hutchinson County at 10. Here they are mowing buffalo grass for hay. We passed a great pile of stones that had been cleared off the land. Saw some good wheat. Mr. Cooley overtook us at 12 o'clock when we came to a Russian settlement. He had not been able to get grain or any feed in Bridgewater though there are three mills in the town.

The Russian settlement—adobe houses, barns and chicken houses, and piles of peat to burn. The houses are back from the road and most of them are built long, the house in one end and the barn in the other. We stopped at one house for water.

We can see timber along the Jim River.* It is only six miles away on our right hand, but 18 miles ahead of us. This is nice country but as one Russian said, "Nix good this year, nix good last year." We carried water in the wagons and camped without water, in a very good place except for that lack. Thermometer at 100° in the wagon.

The road has been almost perfectly level for

---

*The James River

two days, only now and then a small ravine, no hills. Land here is priced from $2,500 to $3,000 a quarter section.*

———

July 21

THOUGHT WE WOULD get an early start but everything went wrong, of course. We are out of bread so baked biscuit, and we made gravy with the chicken we cooked last night, poured it over the biscuits and called it chicken pie. When we were hitching up we let go of old Pet and she started off. Manly† had the halter off Little Pet so she could not go after her mother. I said Whoa and went toward her and as soon as she saw I was coming she ran. I could not catch her. Mr. Cooley chased her on his pony and they were far away before he could head her. She was going to Missouri without waiting for us. We finally got started at 8:20.

We are going gradually down toward the river. It is only 5 miles southwest of us and there is timber thick along its bank. Harvesting and

*A quarter section was 160 acres.
†Laura's name for Almanzo

stacking is done here, and plowing begun.

At 10:30 the bluffs across the Jim River are in sight.

At 12 we crossed the line into Yankton County and now at 2:15 we are on the Jim River flats. And they are flat as a floor. Some grain fields are on them, and meadows, and beside the road are two natural-grown trees, the first we have seen, and little scrubs they are, too.

160 acres of corn are in sight on one side of the road, and 80 on the other.

We have camped on the James River, down among the trees by a water mill. It is a very pleasant place. Only we are not far from a family or settlement of Russians. They all seem to be one family but Manly said he counted 36 children all the same size and Mr. Cooley says there are 50 all under 15 years old. They come down to our camp and stand around and stare at us.

The man who seems to be the head of the tribe, or commune or whatever it is, said they came here five years ago and now they own 17 quarter sections. They have herds of cattle, good horses, and 300 geese.

Just at dusk a boy came with a great big fish and wanted to know if we would pay for it. The men were gone and Emma Cooley and I did not know what it was worth. The boy said we might have it for a dime but Emma and I could not scrape up a dime between us. We were about to give up, when the men came and bought the fish. In a few minutes the boy came back with two smaller ones and wanted 15 cents for them but finally took ten.

We are going to sleep tonight to the sound of running water. Manly killed a snake this eve.

Sunday, July 22

WE ALL TOOK A BATH this morning. Mr. and Mrs. Cooley and the children went into the river. Paul and George had a rope around them and tried to swim. Rose went out with Mrs. Cooley, she had a rope around her and I held on to its end. She went out waist deep and paddled around, and sat down up to her chin.

The Russians have hung around us all day, children and grown folks both. They cannot talk and they understand only a little. They are very kind, they brought milk and a great pan of biscuits, and gave them to us, showing us that they were presents. The biscuits are light and very good. We got to feel a little acquainted with the folks, told them all our names and asked theirs and let them swing in the hammock and sit in the chairs. They are very curious and want to examine everything, talking about it to each other.

They wanted us to come to their houses, so Manly and I went. They showed us the geese and we watched the milkmaids milk. They look like the pictures of German and Russian milkmaids and peasants. Their yellow hair is combed smooth down each side of their faces and hangs in long braids behind and they wear handkerchiefs over their heads. They are all dressed alike. There are no sleeves in the women's long blue calico dresses but under them they wear white shirts with long white sleeves. The men have whiskered cheeks and long golden beards. They wear blue blouses that hang down long, to their knees almost, with belts around their waists. They were all very polite and smiling, seeming to try to say they were glad we came. They gave us another big pail of the fresh warm milk and Manly gave them a fire mat. One man seemed quite Americanized, Manly said to him slowly that the mat will not burn and he said that he understood. He may not believe it but if he tries it he will find out.

When we were leaving a woman opened the front of her dress and took out a baking of cold biscuits from right against her bare skin and gave them to me. The man told me to put them in my shirt, but I carried them in Manly's clean handkerchief instead. The man said it was hard for people to cook when traveling. They are very kind people. A pity to waste the biscuits but we could not eat them.

The Russians have a great huge dog. He was higher than my belt as we stood together and his great head looked like a wolf's, only larger. His ears were trimmed to make them like a wolf's ears and he was a bright brown all over. He was very loving, he rubbed against Rose and me and we put our arms around his big neck. There was a little puppy just like him and Manly tried to buy it but they would not sell.

They have splendid barns and great corncribs and a windmill. Their land runs along the river. Each man works his own land but all of them together own all the stock in common.

We have spent a most pleasant Sunday and we are rested. Paul climbed onto Little Pet's back and the colt did not care, he was gentle.

29

—⁓⁓—

July 23

WE STARTED AT 8. Hated to leave our camping place, it seems quite like home. We crossed the James River and in 20 minutes we reached the top of the bluffs on the other side. We all stopped and looked back at the scene and I wished for an artist's hand or a poet's brain or even to be able to tell in good plain prose how beautiful it was. If I had been the Indians I would have scalped more white folks before I ever would have left it.

We could see the river winding down the valley, the water gleaming through the trees that grow on the bank. Beyond it the bluffs rose high and bare, browned and burned, above the lovely green of trees and grass and the shining water. On this side the bluffs again were gigantic brown waves tumbled and tossed about.

On this side of the James we have passed fields of corn 8 feet high. There are cottonwood hedges along the road, the trees 10 inches through and 35 or 40 feet tall. But it all seems burned and bare after our camping grounds by the river.

10 o'clock. It is 101° in the shade in the wagon, and hardly a breath of air.

At 11 o'clock, 9 miles from Yankton, we stopped at a windmill to water the horses. The man who owned the house told us he paid $5,000, for three 80's, without a building.

Not far from Yankton we crossed a bone-dry creek bed with the most desolate barren bluffs on each side. Covered with stones and the grass dry and brown, they looked like great drifts of sand that somehow had stopped drifting.

We reached Yankton at 4 o'clock. Drove by the insane asylum. The buildings look nice and they stand in the middle of a large farm of acres and acres of corn and potatoes. Manly wanted to stop and go through the asylum but I could not bear to, so we did not. We passed by the Yankton College, the buildings are very nice.

I am greatly disappointed in Yankton, it is a stick in the mud. We drove all over the town to find a little feed for the teams, went to the mill and the elevator and the feed stores, and finally found a couple of sacks of ground feed but not a bit of flax* in the whole town. There were no green

*Flaxseed was indispensable first aid for hurts and minor ills. A boiling-hot flaxseed poultice holds hotter heat longer than a bread-and-milk one, and usually it works better than layers of cold vinegar-and-brown-paper.   R.W.L.

vegetables, nor any figs nor dates in the grocery stores. It would be a blessing to Yankton if Carpenter would move down here, or if folks in Yankton would send to De Smet for what they need. They have a number of elevators, 2 or 3 mills, and 6 feed stores, but we carried the most of the feed away in two sacks.

I got my revolver fixed, then we had to spend so much time hunting for feed all over town that Mr. Cooley got to the ferry first. Mrs. Cooley and Paul crossed the river, then the ferry came back and took Mr. Cooley over. It was leaving just as we drove down to the landing at 6 o'clock and while we were waiting for it to come back a bad-looking storm came up. It was not rain, only wind and dust.

We had to face the river to keep the wagon's back to the wind so that it would not be blown over. The wind lifted the hind wheels twice before Manly could get them roped down. The ferryman did not like to try to cross the river in the storm. He waited on the other side until the blow was over, and we were afraid he would not cross again that night. But he did.*

*When the rear wheels lifted as if the wagon were going end over end into the river, my father jumped out, leaving the reins in my mother's hands. While she held and gentled the nervous horses,

Where we crossed the Missouri it is one mile wide, very nasty and muddy. I do not wonder that it is called The Big Muddy, and since I have seen the dust blowing into it I do not think it strange that it is muddy. The Missouri is nothing like as beautiful as the Jim.

Pet made no fuss at all at the ferry, but drove onto it nicely, stood as quiet as could be, and calmly drove off it. Her colt Little Pet ran onto it loose and stood beside her as still as a mouse.

About a mile from the river we camped in woods. Temperature 98°.

~~~~

July 24

MR. COOLEY GOT UP EARLY and went fishing but did not get a bite. We were all tired from being up so late last night, and did not get started until 9

I craned around the edge of the side-curtain to see what my father was doing. He was driving a picket-pin into the ground, and tying a wheel to it with the picket rope. Behind us was a covered wagon, behind it another, and another. As far as I could see, covered wagons stood one beyond another in a long, long line. Behind them and over them, high over half the sky, a yellow wave of dust was curling and coming. My mother said to me, "That's your last sight of Dakota."   R.W.L.

o'clock. We had taken the wrong road, so we had to go back to the river and start again on the right one. For a little way we followed the river and could see down it, four or five miles across the water. It was a grand sight, though the scenery on the banks is nothing. What is it about water that always affects a person? I never see a great river or lake but I think how I would like to see a world made and watch it through all its changes.

The banks of the Missouri are crumbling all the time and falling into the water. In one place the road had fallen in. There on the river flats before we reached the bluffs we saw 24 hay stacks at one time, and mowing had only begun. Four mowing machines were working. Hay is $9. a ton in Yankton.

Well, we have come to the bluffs. On the side next the river they look as if they had been cut straight down with a knife. Grass has not grown on the face. All along the foot of it trees are growing, sheltered from the south wind. Plums, grapes, black currants and sweet clover grow wild on the bottom land. Sweet clover 8 feet high. And the first oak trees we have seen.

We have been going over the bluffs, the most desolate bare hills I ever saw, without houses or

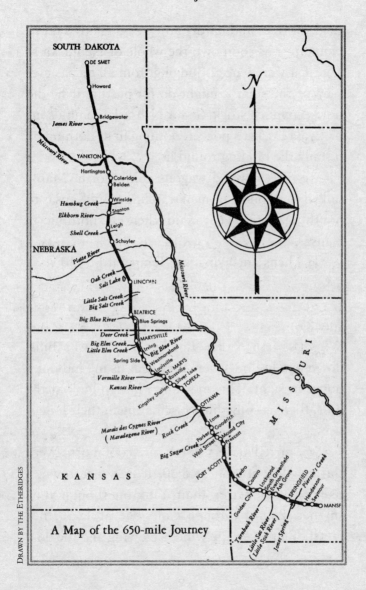

A Map of the 650-mile Journey

fields or trees and hardly any grass. Manly said he would just as soon own the whole of Nebraska as not, if it were fenced. Judging from all he has ever seen of the state it might do for pasture if he did not keep much stock. So far Nebraska reminds me of Lydia Locket's pocket, nothing in it, nothing on it, only the binding round it.

We meet covered wagons going north. Manly talked to a couple of men traveling from Kansas to South Dakota. They said there is nothing in Kansas.

The hens are laying yet. Temperature 110°.

July 25

WE SPENT THE NIGHT among the Nebraska hills, down in a hollow where they shut us in, and not a house in sight. This morning I like to look at the hills, there is something fascinating in their loneliness.

We started at 7:35. It is a nice cool morn. Went through Hartington at 8:30. It is a nice town, I like it much better than Yankton though it is smaller. Passed through Coleridge at 12:30, not much of a place. The wind is blowing and the dust flying till we can hardly see. Talk about hard roads in Dakota, I never saw hard roads till now. The more I see of Nebraska the less I like it. We have been climbing over bluffs all day.

Just south of Coleridge there are 22 families that are going to start for Missouri in about 6 weeks, though this country is very thinly settled. One man said he has lived here for 6 years and has not seen a good crop yet.

We camped east of the town of Belden one mile, but within sight of it, by a creek. Not so much as a bush to be seen. Manly did the chores so Mr. Cooley could go fishing. He caught 11 fish. Temperature 109°.

The man living near where we camped is working for a man in Sioux City who owns 3,000 acres of land here, in a body. 500 acres of it are in pasture and 250 in meadow.

July 26

MR. COOLEY WENT FISHING again this morning and caught 2. We were on the road at 8:40. There has been plenty of rain right here and crops are good, corn, wheat and oats. But three miles west they have nothing. Land is $25 an acre here.

Met a load of emigrants at noon. They are going north. Thermometer 110° in shade.

This afternoon we met a family of emigrants, man, woman and two children. They had been to Missouri and are coming back. They started from Moody County, Dakota, the 8th of May and went to Taney County, Missouri. They stayed only 10 days and started back, have been on the road ever since. They would not live in Missouri if you gave them the whole of it. "Why, hardly any of the houses have windows in them, just holes, and lots of the women have never seen a railroad train nor an organ," and the land is awful stony. They think of stopping in Cedar County, Nebraska.

Crops are poor since noon, country about as dry as Dakota. Went through Winside about 4 o'clock. Roads are awfully hilly and Mr. Cooley wishes we had kept farther west and gone to Columbus instead of Schuyler.

Crossed Humbug Creek and camped by the first house south. The people are Germans and very nice, they gave us milk. Humbug Creek and Winside are well named only they should have spelled it Windside. We have faced a hot hard wind all day.

~~~

July 27

STARTED AT 8:15. We have gone through Cedar
County and nearly through Wayne County,
Nebraska. We cannot tell when we come to a
county line as we could in Dakota, the roads pay
no attention to section lines but wander up and
down and around the hills.

The soil in Wayne County is very fine and
close, not exactly clay but clayey. The people here
claim it is the best soil on earth to stand drought.

Crossed the line into Stanton County at 9.
There are large pastures and the grain fields are all
fenced. A good many sleek cattle are in sight.
Cornfields are 3 miles long and as far back as you
can see. There are a few groves. Wind blows hard
but cool this morning.

At 10:20 we saw *an orchard with apples*.

The hills are covered with corn as far as eye can
see, acres and acres of corn. Lots of groves. Nearly
all the people are Germans. One gave Manly two
large apples off his trees. He has a large orchard
and the trees hang full.

Just passed a house where the man owns 540
acres of land and has 300 hogs.

A little farther on, a farm of 500 acres. The owner had 450 hogs and only 50 bushels of old corn. He says if it does not rain within 24 hours the tassels on the new crop will dry and he will not harvest a kernel of corn. The corn looks nice to us but I suppose the farmers here know. Their wheat only sold for 32 cents last year and it is 32 cents now.

We came into the Elkhorn valley at 1:45 and it is pretty, very level, with many groves and nice houses and natural timber along the river.

An emigrant team is behind us and every minute I expect to hear the usual, Where did you come from? Where are you going? How are the crops up your way? This never—hardly ever—fails.

Found an ear of corn 10 inches long, $7^1/_2$ inches around.

Arrived at Stanton at 3 P.M. It is a good looking town, large pretty buildings, clean big houses with trees. People mostly Germans. German signs on the stores and German texts on the churches. Wheat is going 16 to 20 bushels to the acre. Corn is killed by the hot wind. Yesterday it was 126° in the shade here in Stanton.

Crossed the Elkhorn river on a bridge. A few miles farther on we camped by the side of the road in the shade of some trees. There was a gang of horse traders on the river and we did not want to camp near them.

———w———

July 28

WE WASHED THIS MORNING, or rather Mrs. Cooley did out a washing and I washed 4 garments. I wash out most of the clothes in a pail as they get dirty so I do not have washings. The neighbors sent us a pailful of delicious cold milk, out of the water where they keep it for the creamery.

The washing had to dry, so we did not start to travel until after dinner. The roads are awful killers for the horses. We had gone about 3 miles when we missed the Cooleys' dog. Mr. Cooley wanted to go on but Mrs. Cooley would not. Finally it was decided that he would go back to look for her and the rest of us would go on.

We took the ridge road, not to go up and down the hills, so we followed along the top of the ridge through acres and acres of corn fields. We could see nothing of Mr. Cooley when it was time to camp, but we camped by the side of the road on the prairie. There was good grass for the horses and a pump in a pasture, just through the fence.

We got the horses watered and picketed out, when here came Mr. Cooley over a hill from the south. An old Bohemian had come out and would not let him cross a field where we had gone, so he had to go all around to come back to us. He had found the dog where we camped last night.

The oats and wheat are good here and the corn does not look bad but of course it needs rain so people are blue and cross and stingy.

There are wild strawberry plants here, and rattlesnakes.

Sunday, July 29

COOKED BREAKFAST and bathed and lay around in the shade of the wagons. Temperature 96°. Rested all day and went to bed early.

July 30

STARTED AT 8 and crossed the line into Colfax County twenty minutes later. Went through Leigh at 10 o'clock, a lively little town that has not outgrown the country.

Crops are still the same but roads are not so hilly.

We camped on the bank of Shell Creek in the woods. A lovely place, even better than our camp on the Jim River. The children and Mrs. Cooley and I went wading. The bank was so steep that we had to steady each other down, and pull and push each other up. We paddled and played in the rippling cool water. Rose sat down in it, splash! We found two large live clams.

July 31

THE WIND BLEW terribly in the night. We were thankful for the shelter of the trees. It must have rained hard somewhere, for the creek rose 8 inches.

Started at 9. We are following down the valley of the creek on a nice level road.

Reached Schuyler at noon, all the way on the level road. Here we had to get the tires set, so we did not leave town till 3. I met an interesting woman. She drove up to the wagon in a buggy and began by asking if it isn't hot to be traveling. I liked her and we talked a long time. Her husband owns a large farm north of Schuyler but they are going back to the West Indies in a few weeks. They are Canadians but her husband was in the West Indies as a boy and they have spent half their lives there. They thought they would like to live here but do not like it as well as they expected, so they will rent the farm again and she thinks they will stay in the West Indies when they get there. She said it is a monotonous life but very pleasant, the servants do all the work. She wanted to know all about Dakota and everything she said was sensible. She is an elderly lady, and I think Scotch.

South of Schuyler the land is sandy, two miles to La Platte River. We crossed the Platte on a bridge half a mile long, humped in the middle so we went up and down hill on it. The river is full of sand bars that keep shifting.

Half a mile beyond it we camped in a grove of willows. The Cooleys lingered in town and had not arrived when we camped. Manly and I hurried our supper and left Rose to watch the camp while we "hit the dust" back to the river so I could go wading in daylight.

The water was clear, warm and soft. The sand was soft and warm but shifting. It ran away right under my feet while I waded, or if I stood still it drifted over them. For fun I stood still until my feet were covered. As Manly said, we "hit the dust" going, but we "packed sand" coming back.

On the way back we saw a snake and two large

toads. We went into a pasture to look at some trees. The sand had drifted away from them until the tree trunks stood up higher than my head, tiptoe on their bare, gnarled roots. I could walk under those trees, between their roots, by stooping just a little.

August 1
IT RAINED A LITTLE in the night. We started at 8:40 and the road was level till noon but terribly hilly all the afternoon. We camped by Oak Creek in a little natural glade among the oaks, the best camp yet.

August 2
STARTED LATE because of a lame horse, one of Mr. Cooley's. They had to take care of her foot. We met a team of movers going to work out the railroad tax.* Camped early, only a little way from Oak Creek.

---

*I suppose this was a local or state tax to pay a subsidy to a railroad builder. Railroads were the fastest, most modern transportation. The Lincoln administration began to subsidize them from taxes in the 1860's. States and localities, even small towns, followed the example eagerly in the 1880's–90's. "Working out taxes" at $1 a day was usual.   R.W.L.

The wooden bridge across the Platte River, Schuyler,
Nebraska, as it looked when we crossed it.   R.W.L.

~~~~%%~~~~

August 3

STARTED AT 9. Good level road into Lincoln, the capital of Nebraska and a beautiful large city. It is two miles from the first hotel to the post office. The County Court House and the Capitol are grand buildings, and so is the penitentiary. We saw two prisoners in their striped clothes standing outside the gate in the wall. A carload of new barrels was on a sidetrack beside them, I suppose made by the prisoners. A high stone wall surrounds several buildings and joins the back of the main building. Smaller buildings inside the wall look like workshops, one like a foundry.

Eight emigrant wagons trailed our three through several streets of the city. There are motor street cars in Lincoln. Pet and Little Pet were not afraid of them but they scared Mrs. Cooley's team so that they plunged up a bank and nearly upset her wagon.* But it came out all right.

---

*Paul was not allowed to drive through cities and other dangerous places. His mother came back to their second wagon then and took the lines and the responsibility away from him. He was humiliated and I felt hotly (in silence) this injustice to him. He drove the big team perfectly all the rest of the way. George rode with him, but Paul was responsible for the second team and wagon.   R.W.L.

We crossed 11 creeks today, or one creek 11 times, I don't know which, and we passed Salt Lake north west of Lincoln. We are camped about a mile from the penitentiary. Temperature 74°.

August 4

ON THE ROAD AT 7:45, a nice level road and good farms fenced with board fences. We are following the telegraph wires to Beatrice, then do not follow the railroad but go across country.

We have crossed Little Salt Creek and Big Salt Creek. Orchards are as common here as houses. Manly traded one fire mat for a whole bushel of large ripe apples. Plums are nearly ripe. Crops look splendid to us but everyone tells Manly that they are very poor and will make no grain to mention. We passed the best field of oats that Manly ever saw.

Made a hard long drive to get to a good camp, and when we got there we found the creek dry and no grass but plenty of sand burs.* Camped in the edge of a town.

*A sandbur is a weed that grows in inhospitable soil.

Sunday, August 5

SAME AS LAST Sunday. Saw five emigrant wagons. Lost the thermometer.

August 6

STARTED AT 8:30 and reached Beatrice at noon. Corn all dried up and no ears on it. Oats and wheat threshed and a great deal of plowing done.

Beatrice is not as large as Lincoln but a nice town, I think. We saw the courthouse, it is handsome.

Splendid roads all day. We crossed Blue River just south of Beatrice, drove through Blue Springs at 5 in the afternoon and crossed Blue River again. Did not see much of the city because we drove along the north edge and down the east side past a big mill run by water-power. The river runs east of the town, a very pretty river. I do not mention orchards any more because they are common here, there are so many of them.

We saw 8 acres of seedling apple trees about 12 inches high near Blue Springs. Today has been quite cool, but with a little too much wind.

August 7

ON THE ROAD AT 7:30, we crossed the line into
Kansas at 10:28¼ exactly. Judging from what we
have seen and heard of Nebraska, the southeast
corner is quite a good country, but taken as a
whole it is "nix good." I don't like Nebraska.

Crossed Deer Creek at 11 o'clock. At 4 in the
afternoon we came to Marysville, the county seat
of Marshall County, on the Blue River. Here there
is a watermill, capacity 300 barrels a day. We saw
many nice houses and two palatial residences in
the town. Around one is a massive brick fence
about 5 feet high, thick and strong looking. On
each side of the front gate a large granite lion is
crouching, and on each side of the side gate a large
granite dog is lying down.

Beyond Marysville we saw an acre of sweet
potatoes, large dark green leaves on vines covering
the ground.

We drove 27 miles today and camped near a
house where there were two men drunk. They had
lost the bars off their wagon, wanted to trade
horses, etc. Manly had a time getting rid of them
without offense.

52

*Marysville, Kansas. This is a "German Day" parade,
which may have taken place in the year we were there.*

                                                    R.W.L.

August 8

STARTED AT 8:30. Soon crossed Little Elm Creek and Big Elm Creek and drove through beautiful woods of elm, oak, ash, hickory, butternut and walnut. Wild plums, grapes and currants are abundant, and briars and wild flowers of all kinds. A rich sight.

Crossed Blue River again, a lovely river, so clean always, and fresh and cool. We crossed it on a bridge. This bridge is about 300 feet long. Irving is a tiny small town but it has an Opera House with a round roof, it looks like an engine boiler.

Then we crossed the Blue again. Every time we cross it, it is lovelier than before. Improved land here is from $15. to $25. an acre. Could buy an 80 on the Blue bottoms, well improved, for $3,000. The bottom land is all good farms. The bluffs are stony.

We camped near Spring Side, well named. There are springs on every side. I got water from a spring that boils up out of solid rock, cool and clear.

August 9

STARTED AT 8:30. Awfully hilly roads, and stony. We saw a milk-house built of stone with a spring running through it, a splendid thing. Land in Pottawatomie County is $4. an acre up.

Camped in the edge of Westmoorland, the county seat. At supper time we had company, some men, two women, and children. They are regular southerners, camped near by, traveling north. To Nebraska or maybe Dakota, looking for work.

———⚍———

August 10
STARTED AT 8:30 and drove through the driest country we have seen since leaving Dakota. Went through Louisville, drove 3 miles farther and camped on the bank of Vermille River,* some call it Stony Creek.

———⚍———

August 12
TODAY WAS NOT as monotonous as common. 3 emigrant wagons passed us going south, and one going north. Manly and Mr. Cooley took turns talking to the people. Five wagons were going to Missouri or Arkansas, one to Arkansas, one to Indian Territory.

We had a good camping place on a little headland by the river. I rode Little Pet awhile, bareback, not going anywhere—she was turned loose to feed. Two emigrants talked to me, a young man and his

---

*The Vermillion River

mother in their wagon. They used to live in Missouri, went to Colorado, are now going back to Missouri to stay.

—◦∼◦—

August 13

DROVE THROUGH ST. MARY'S. A pleasant town but strange, it is altogether southern, and Catholic. There is a beautiful large church with a pure white marble Saint Mary above the wide doors and two white marble statues of Mother and Child in the yard. The houses are neat and pretty. It is a clean town.

We drove to the top of a little bluff to look over the Kansas River, and there on the bottom lands we saw cornfields stretching as far as the eye could reach. Manly said he should think there were a thousand acres in sight.

On our way Manly went to a farmhouse to trade a fire mat for some green corn for our supper, and we had an invitation to stay to dinner and put our horses in the barn and feed them. The woman came out to make me welcome. Such nice people, and a nice place, everything well kept up. Of course we could not stay. We could not be neighborly to them in return and we must get to Missouri and settled before winter.

At noon we went through Rossville, a small place, but just as we were going by the depot the train came in. The engine frightened Prince and he went through a barb-wire fence. He struck it straight and went right through it, end over end, jumped up, ran against a clothesline and broke that and ran back to the fence. He stopped when Manly said, "Whoa, Prince," and Manly helped him through the wire. He had only one mark, a cut about an inch long where a barb had struck him. How he ever got through so well is a wonder.

Watermelons are ripe and plentiful. Manly and Mr. Cooley bought big ones for 5 cents. We stopped by the road in the shade of trees and all of us had all the watermelon we could eat.

We passed Kingsley Station, 80 miles west of Kansas City, Missouri, and 558 miles east of Denver, Colorado. Went through Silver Lake. The lake itself is south of the town; it is 4 miles long and a half a mile wide, and trees are all around it. There is a place where a man rents boats.

We camped in a schoolhouse yard. There was a hedge all around it and a pump by the house, beside a sycamore tree. Two families going by in covered wagons stopped for water. They had been to Missouri and were going back home to dispose of their property in Nebraska, then they are moving to Missouri.

It is *terribly* dusty. We breathe dust all day and everything is covered thick with it.

————————

August 14

STARTED AT 8:30. Dust is 3 to 5 inches deep on the road and the breeze is on our backs so all the time we are in a smother of dust. Along the roads are hedges of Osage Orange trees, 20 or 30 feet high, set close together. They are thorny. Their fruit is like green oranges, but no good for eating nor for anything else.

We stopped to eat dinner about a mile from Topeka, then drove on through the city. There are a great many colored people in and around it. In North Topeka the street cars are electric, in South Topeka they are motor cars.

The streets are asphaltum pavement and it is lovely to drive on, so soft and quiet that it doesn't seem real. It gives like rubber to the horses' feet. The caulks on their shoes make dents in it and slowly the dents fill up till the place is smooth again.

We drove a block out of our way to see the

Capitol, where they had that war in the legislature. The building is handsome but the grounds are all unkempt, not finished at all.

We crossed the Kansas River on an iron bridge that must be 400 or 500 feet long. The river is like the Platte, not quite as wide but full of sand bars.

South of Topeka a man gave us some late daily papers. He has 240 acres here but his home is in Colorado. He has mining interests there. He told Manly that the fuss over silver in Washington has made him lose $1,000,000.

We camped by the side of a church, in dust.

———— ✺ ————

August 15
STARTED AT 7:20. Found a little black-and-tan dog in the road, lost. He is skin and bones, must have been starving, and is afraid of us. We stopped at several houses to ask, but nobody knew where he belonged so we are taking him along. The children delight to feed him milk. We have named him Fido.

Today I saved a horse chestnut, and we came to hazelnuts for the first time.

Went through Richland at noon. We drove past the church. There was a Sunday School picnic on the church grounds.

Kansas Avenue in Topeka, Kansas, as it looked when
we passed through.   R.W.L.

We camped by a schoolhouse in the southwest corner of Douglas County. There was good grass for the teams and a pump gushed out delicious cold, clear water. This is the best farming country we have seen yet, prairie with natural groves here and there and timber along the creeks.

As we came along the road Manly sold and traded a good many fire mats, and one farmer wanted to rent him a farm for a third of the crops. Another came to us at the schoolhouse where we camped, and wanted us to stay here and rent. We are going on to Missouri but may come back here if we do not like it there. Land here is worth $20. to $40. an acre.

August 16

ON OUR WAY AT 7:25. Fido is quite friendly this morning. He still seems sad but he has stopped trembling and seems content to sit in my lap and look at the country we are passing. The wheat crop is bountiful here and the corn crop is pretty good. There is a coal bank where men mine the coal and sell all they dig for $1.25 a ton.

At 5 in the afternoon we came through Ottawa.

There is a North and a South Ottawa, separated by the Maradegene* River. They are the county seat of Franklin County. The men of Ottawa stole the county seat in the night, from another town, and for some time they had to guard it with the militia, to keep it. The courthouse is quite an imposing building.

The Sante Fe Railroad hospital is in the north edge of North Ottawa, a large brick building. It looks very clean. In South Ottawa there is a handsome college building made of the native stone. In all the towns now there are many colored people.

We camped on the bank of Rock Creek in the suburbs of South Ottawa. Two men coming by stopped and looked at Prince for some time and as they went on the elderly one said to the other, "That is the nicest colt I have seen for years." The hens are laying yet.

August 17
FIDO IS A GOOD WATCH DOG. He growls at every stranger who comes to the wagon, and at night at everyone that passes.

*Real name of this river is Marais des Cygnes, which means "Marshland of the Swans."

We started at 7:30. The wild morning-glories are rioting everywhere, all colors like the tame ones. We passed a large field of castor beans. They are raised here as a crop, they run 10 to 15 bushels to the acre and sell for $1.25 to $1.50 a bushel. They are picked every two weeks, piled up in the sun till they pop open, then run through a fanning mill and sacked.

We reached Lane at 4 o'clock and had old Pet shod. The blacksmith came from Kentucky two years ago and looks just like the pictures of a Kentucky man. He has 130 acres of bottom land running down to Pottawatomie River, and a stone house as large as any house in De Smet. It is very handsome and perfectly finished. The house stands on Main Street in Lane and the land lies northwest from it. He is going back to Kentucky and wants to sell. Asks $4300. for shop, house and land.

South of Lane we stopped at a farmhouse to ask for water and the woman said she did not have enough to spare but we could get plenty "over yon way."

Camped again by a schoolhouse and pump. Washed out some things after supper. They dry overnight.

August 18

STARTED AT 7 THIS MORNING, went through Parker and came to Goodrich at noon. They are both small places and the country around them is not as good as we have been seeing. The people say they never have the rain here that others get farther north.

Camped by Big Sugar Creek, up on its high bank in the woods beside the road.

———

Sunday, August 19

MR. COOLEY'S STOVE had worked loose. He and Manly had to fix it so it will ride. Mrs. Cooley and I and the children went down to the creek and found some mussels and some clam shells. A woman and 2 children came to see us. They come from Missouri and they are camping near by on their way to Nebraska.

———

August 20

GOT A GOOD START AT 7:30 but the roads are awfully stony. Crops are poor. Everyone tells us they never get rain here when they need it. We went through Wall Street, it is nothing but a little country store.

At noon we came to Mound City which is quite a city. We bought bread and an 8-cent pie and 2 cents worth of tomatoes. Tomatoes are 30 cents a bushel.

We stopped to eat dinner in the shade of a tree beside the road. Three emigrant wagons passed while we were eating. Two were going to Missouri and one coming back. This afternoon we saw three more, one going to Missouri, one coming back. Manly did not ask the other.

Water has been scarce all day and what little we found tasted so bad we could not get a good drink. It is clear and clean but it feels slick and tastes bitter, it spoils the taste of tea. The horses have to be very thirsty to take it.

Camped beside the road on the prairie. Bought a little hay and could get only a little water. Looks like rain.

August 21

IT RAINED HARD most of the night and was still pouring down when time came to get up. Manly put on his rubber coat, started the fire and put water on to heat, then fed our horses. By that time the rain was no more than a drizzle so I got out and made breakfast. We ate in the wagon, out of the wet.

Roads are muddy but sky is clear overhead. We went through Prescott, only a little station. Met a family of emigrants who have spent the last two months traveling in southwest Missouri. They do not like it at all down there. The man said, "Right there is the place to go if a man wants to bury himself from the world and live on hoecake and clabber," and the woman agreed with him.

We passed another covered wagon stopped by the road, and those folks are on their way to Missouri. The whole country is just full of emigrants, going and coming. Fort Scott seemed to be crowded with them. We reached Fort Scott at 6 o'clock, and a man there said that 15 emigrant wagons went along that street yesterday.

Fort Scott is a bower of trees. The houses look clean and contented; the business buildings are handsome. The country around Fort Scott looks like it might be a very good country. Crops are good where there are any, but there is lots of idle land and many places are gone back.* It seems that the people are shiftless; but you never can tell. A man said this

---

*Laura meant that the land wasn't being farmed anymore.

The main street of Fort Scott, Kansas, as it looked in the late 1880's.   R.W.L.

country is worthless, and when Manly said that it looked to him like good land, he said, Oh yes, the land will raise anything that's planted but if you can't sell what you raise for enough to pay back the cost of raising it, what's the land worth?

Coal is lying around on top of the ground and cropping out of every bank. At the coal mines, or coal banks as they call them, the coal is worth $5. a bushel.

We received 3 letters at Fort Scott, 2 from home. A little way south of the city we camped beside the road.

August 22

A GOOD START AT 7:15 and this morning we are driving through pretty country. Crops look good. Oats are running 30 to 60 bushels to the acre, wheat from 10 to 30. All the wood you want can be had for the hauling and coal is delivered at the house for $1.25 a ton. Land is worth from $10. an acre up, unimproved, and $15. to $25. when well improved, 12 miles from Fort Scott.

Exactly at 2:24$^3/_4$ P.M. we crossed the line into Missouri. And the very first cornfield we saw beat even those Kansas cornfields.

We met 7 emigrant wagons leaving Missouri. One family had a red bird, a mockingbird, and a lot of canaries in cages hung under the canvas in the wagon with them. We had quite a chat and heard the mockingbird sing. We camped by a house in the woods.

August 23

STARTED OUT AT 7:30. The country looks nice this morning. At 9:35 we came to Pedro, a little town on one side of the railroad tracks, and just across the tracks on the other side is the town of Liberal. A man in Pedro told us that one of the finest countries in the world will be around Mansfield.

In the late afternoon we went through Lamar, the nicest small city we have seen, 2,860 inhabitants. It is all so clean and fresh, all the streets set out to shade trees.

We camped among oak trees, not far from a camp of emigrants from Kentucky. Beautiful sturdy oak trees on both sides of the road.

August 24

ON THE ROAD bright and early, 7:20. Weather cool and cloudy, looks like rain. Went through Canova in the morning. It is a little place. At noon we were going through Golden City, a nicer little place. The country looks good, but judging from weeds in the gardens and fields, the people are shiftless. This is a land of many springs and clear brooks. Some of the earth is yellow and some is red. The road is stony often.

Went through another little town, Lockwood, at 4 o'clock, and camped by a swift-running little creek of the clearest water. It is most delicious water to drink, cold, with a cool, snappy flavor.

Except in the towns, we have seen only one schoolhouse so far in Missouri.

We drove in the rain this afternoon, for the first time since we left Dakota. It was a good steady pouring rain, but we kept dry in the wagon and the rain stopped before camping time.

—⁓—

August 25

LEFT CAMP AT 7:35. It rained again in the night and the road was muddy but after a few miles we came to country where it did not rain so the road was dry. The uplands are stony but there are good bottomland farms. Much timber is in sight, oaks, hickories, walnuts, and there are lots of wild crabapples, plums and thorn apples.

In South Greenfield two land agents came out and wanted us to stop here. One was C. C. Akin, the man who located Mr. Sherwin. He said Mr. Sherwin was here only a week ago, has just gone. Mr. Sherwin looked Wright County over thoroughly and came back to Cedar County and located here. But finally Mr. Akin said there is just as good land in Wright County as Mr. Sherwin bought.

Well, we are in the Ozarks at last, just in the beginning of them, and they are beautiful. We passed along the foot of some hills and could look up their sides. The trees and rocks are lovely. Manly says we could almost live on the looks of them.

We stopped for dinner just before we came to the prettiest part, by the side of a swiftly running stream, Turnback River. We forded it, through the shallow water all rippling and sparkling.

There was another clear stream to cross before we came to Everton at 5 o'clock. Here we stopped to get the horses shod but there was not time to shoe them all today, so we camped by a creek in the edge of town for over Sunday.

———※———

Sunday, August 26

A DAY FOR WRITING, reading, sleeping. We let the children wade in the shallow creek, within our sight. I spent almost the whole time writing to the home folks about the country since Fort Scott and these hills and woods.

———※———

August 27

OUT OF CAMP AT 7:10. We like this country. A man tried to get us to settle just across the road from him, said we could buy that 40 for $700. It was good land.

We forded Little Sock* River and came through Ash Grove, a lively little town noted for its lime kiln. Two new brick blocks are going up on Main Street.

Camped 12 miles from Springfield. Manly was unhitching the team when a man with his wife and daughter in a covered wagon drove up and wanted to know where he could water his mules. They live 14 miles east of Springfield in Henderson County and were going to visit the

*Real name of river is Little Sac.

woman's brother in Ash Grove.

After we had talked awhile they said they would like to camp by us if we could sell them a little meat to cook. They had not intended to camp and had brought nothing to eat. We let them have some meat and they used our camp stove, so we got quite well acquainted. They are good, friendly folks. Their name is Davis. After the chores were done they brought over a large watermelon and we called the Cooleys to come, and all of us ate the whole big melon. You can buy a 20-lb. watermelon here for 5 cents.

August 28

LEFT CAMP AT 6:28. Good road from Ash Grove all the way to Springfield, not hilly nor very stony. This is the Ozark plateau and the country looks much like prairie country though there are groves and timber always along the streams.

Arrived in Springfield at 9:25. It is a thriving city with fine houses and four business blocks stand around a town square. The stores are well stocked and busy. Manly hitched the horses and we bought shoes for Rose and myself, a calico dress for me, and a new hat for Manly. It did not take much time and we drove right along through the city. We were out of it before noon. It has 21,850 inhabitants, and is the nicest city we have seen yet. It is simply grand.

We could see two straight miles down Walnut Street, a very little down grade, with large shade trees on each side, large handsome residences, and the pavement as smooth and clean as can be.

Five miles east of Springfield is Jones Spring. The water is clear as glass, and it comes pouring out of a cave in a ledge of rock. At its mouth the cave is 4 feet high and 10 feet wide, and nobody knows how far back it goes. Manly and Mr. Cooley went quite a distance back into it and threw stones as far as they could throw them, and the stones fell plunk into water far back in the dark.

The water pours out of the cave 14 inches deep and runs away over the stones among the trees, a lively little creek.

We were told that 7 miles southeast of Jones Spring a stream comes out of a cave so large that you can keep rowing a boat back into it for half a day.

After crossing Pierson's Creek we met, one right after another, 10 emigrant wagons leaving Missouri. We camped in the edge of Henderson, a little inland town, on the bank of a spring brook.

⟨⟨⟨

August 29

LEFT CAMP AT 7:10. We are driving along a lovely road through the woods, we are shaded by oak trees. The farther we go, the more we like this country. Parts of Nebraska and Kansas are well enough but Missouri is simply glorious. There Manly interrupted me to say, "This is beautiful country."

The road goes up hill and down, and it is rutted and dusty and stony but every turn of the wheels changes our view of the woods and the hills. The sky seems lower here, and it is the softest blue. The distances and the valleys are blue whenever you can see them. It is a drowsy country that makes you feel wide awake and alive but somehow contented.

We went through a little station on the railroad and a few miles farther on we came to a fruit farm of 400 acres. A company owns it. There are 26,000 little young trees already set out in rows striping the curves of the land, and the whole 400 acres will be planted as soon as possible. Acres of strawberries and other small fruit are in bearing. We stopped to look our fill of the sight and Manly fell into conversation with some of the company's men. They told him of a 40 he can buy for $400, all cleared and into grass except five acres of woods, and with a good ever-flowing spring, a comfortable log house and a barn.

We drove through Seymour in the late afternoon. The Main Streets of towns here are built around open squares, with the hitching posts surrounding the square. In the office of the Seymour paper, the *Enterprise*, a girl was setting type. A man spoke to us, who had lived years in Dakota, near Sioux Falls, he has a brother living there now. He is farming near Seymour. He said the climate here can't be beat, we never will want to leave these hills, but it will take us some time to get used to the stones.

Oh no, we are not out of the world nor behind the times here in the Ozarks. Why, even the cows know "the latest." Two of them feeding along the road were playing Ta-ra-ra *Boom!* de-ay! The little cow's bell rang Ta-ra-ra, then the bigger cow's bell clanged, *Boom!* de-ay. I said, "What is that tune they are playing?" and we listened. It was as plain as could be, tones and time and all, and so comical. We drove on singing Ta-ra-ra *Boom!* de-ay! along the road.

We passed several springs and crossed some little brooks. The fences are snake fences of split logs and all along them, in the corners, fruit grows wild. There are masses of blackberries, and seedling peaches and plums and cherries, and luscious-looking fruits ripening in little trees that I don't know,* a lavishness of fruit growing wild. It seems to be free for the taking.

We could not reach Mansfield today. Camped by a spring 10½ miles short of it. In no time at all Rose and I filled a quart pail with big juicy blackberries. They are growing wild in big patches in the woods, ripening and falling off and wasting.

Six more emigrant wagons camped around the spring before dark. Seasoned oak wood, sawed, split and delivered and corded, brings $1. a cord here.

August 30, 1894
HITCHED UP AND GOING AT 7:10. The road is rough and rocky through the ravines but not so bad between them and there are trees all the way.

We are passing through the Memphis fruit

---

*These were wild persimmons and pawpaws.   R.W.L.

Mansfield, Missouri, as it looked about 1894. This picture was probably taken on Memorial Day or on the Fourth of July.

farms, 1,500 acres, part of the way on both sides of the road. It is a young orchard, rows upon rows of little trees, apple and peach, curving over the plowed hills.

Some covered wagons came up behind us and we came up behind some ahead, all the teams going slowly, holding back down hill and pulling up hill. At 11:30 we came into Mansfield in a long line of 10 emigrant wagons.

Mansfield is a good town of 300 or 400 inhabitants in a good central location where it should grow fast. The railroad runs on one side of the square and two stagecoach lines go from the depot, one south to the county seat of Douglas County, the other north to the county seat of Wright County. There is everything here already that one could want though we must do our worshipping without a Congregational church. There is a Methodist church and a Presbyterian. There is a good school. Around the square, two general stores, two drug stores, the bank, a Boston Racket store, livery stable, blacksmith shop near. There are several nice large houses in big yards with trees. South of the tracks is as good as north of them; two or three big houses, and a flour mill is there by a mill pond.

Camped in the woods in the western edge of town and this afternoon Manly looked over one place for sale but it was not exactly suited.

Three

Here my mother's record ends. Fifty years later I began casually to speak of our camp in those vanished woods and she stopped the words in my mouth with a fierce, "I don't want to *think* of it!"

I do not remember how many days my father spent hunting for land that the secret hundred dollar bill would buy. Every morning he rode away with some land agent to limp up and down the hills and to come back at evening, nothing found yet.

Paul and George and I were joyous. After the long boredom of so many dull days that we hardly remembered De Smet, now every day was Sunday without Sunday's clean clothes and staid behavior. The camp was a Sunday camp; the Cooleys' wagons on one side, ours on the other; in the grove between them the table and chairs were set and the hammock hung in the shade. The camp stove stood a little way apart over cooling ashes. Farther away the horses were tied under the trees, and behind the wagons were screened places for our Saturday baths.

We had to stay within sight or at least within hearing if our mothers called us, but as soon as morning tasks were done we were free to play in the woods. All day we climbed trees, picked berries, ate unripe walnuts and hazelnuts, cracked between two stones. We startled rabbits that we must not chase far; we watched squirrels and birds, beetles and anthills. The hot air was full of good smells of rotting logs, dusty weeds, damp underneaths of mats of last year's oak leaves. Dandelion stems curled bitter on my tongue's tip and the green curls wilted over my ears.

Sharp flat stones were thick underfoot; we stubbed our toes on them and all our big toes were wrapped in rags. Stone-bruises on our summer-callused heels didn't stop our running. We found toadstools and mosses like teeny-tiniest forests, flat greenish-gray lichen on rocks, little perfect skins of locusts, empty, thin and brittle, clinging with tiny claws to the bark of trees.

We picked up strange stones. When I showed my father a thin triangular one, wavy all over and sharp-pointed, he said it was an Indian arrowhead. We collected dozens of them and Paul found a stone ax-head.

One day I had to stay in camp with Mrs. Cooley, I was told I must mind her and not go out of her sight. My father had found a place, my mother was going with him to see it, and they wanted no worry about me while they were gone. There never had been such a long morning. I was embarrassed and so was Mrs. Cooley. When at last I saw the team coming, my father and mother coming back, I felt like exploding; I could hardly be still and not speak until spoken to.

My father was glowing and my mother shining. She never had talked so fast. Just what they wanted, she told Mrs. Cooley, so much, much more than they'd hoped for. A year-round spring of the best water you ever drank, a snug log house, in woods, on a hill, only a mile and a half from town so Rose could walk to school, and to cap all, just think! four hundred young apple trees, heeled in,* all ready to set out when the land was cleared. They'd bought it, as soon as dinner was over they were going to the bank to sign the papers. We were moving out that afternoon.

When he was excited my father always held himself quiet and steady, moving and speaking with deliberation. Sometimes my quick mother flew out at him, but this day she was soft and warm. She left him eating at the camp table, told me to clear it and wash the dishes when he was through, and went into the screened place to get ready to meet the banker.

I perched on a stump and watched her brush out her hair and braid it. She had beautiful hair, roan-brown, very fine and thick. Unbraided, it shimmered down to her heels; it was so long that when it was tightly braided she could sit on the braids. Usually it hung down her back in one wide braid, but when she dressed up she must put up her hair and endure the headache.

Now she wound the braid around and around into a big mass on the back of her head, and fastened it with her tortoise-shell pins. She fluffed her

*The trees were temporarily set into the soil.

88

bangs into a soft little mat in front, watching her comb in the small looking glass fastened to a tree, and suddenly I realized that she was whistling; I remembered that I hadn't heard her whistling lately.

"Whistling girls and crowing hens always come to some bad ends," she'd say gaily. She was whistling always. She whistled like a bird whistling a tune, clear and soft, clear and sweet, trilling, chirping, or dropping notes one by one as a meadow lark drops them from the sky. I was pleased to hear her whistling again.

Whistling, she buttoned up her new shoes with the buttonhook. She took off her calico dress and folded it neatly. Standing in her bleached muslin petticoats and corset cover trimmed with crocheted lace, she took her best dress, her black cloth wedding dress, out of the box in which it had traveled from Dakota. Whistling "Oh Susanna, don't you cry for me," she put on the skirt and smoothed the placket. I was sorry that the skirt hid her new shoes. She coaxed her arms into the basque's tight sleeves and carefully buttoned all the glittery jet buttons up its front to her chin. With her gold pin she pinned the fold of ribbon, robin's-egg blue, to the front of the stand-up collar. Then, the very last thing, the climax: she pinned on her black sailor hat with the blue ribbon around the crown and the spray of wheat standing straight up at one side. The braids in back tilted the hat forward just a little; in front, the narrow brim rested on the mat of bangs.

She looked lovely; she was beautiful. You could see my father think so, when she came out and he looked at her.

She told him to hurry or they'd be late, but she spoke as if she were singing, not cross at all. He went into the screened place to change his shirt and comb his hair and mustache, and put on his new hat. To me my mother said that I could clear the table now, be sure to wash every dish while they were gone and, as usual, she told me to be careful not to break one. I never had broken a dish.

I remember all this so clearly because of what happened. I had taken away the dishes and wiped the table. My mother put down on it her clean handkerchief and her little red cloth pocketbook with the mother-of-pearl sides; she was wearing her kid gloves. Carefully she brought the writing desk and set it on the table. She laid back its slanted upper half and lifted out the narrow wooden tray that held the pen and the inkwell.

The hundred dollar bill was gone.

There was a shock, like stepping in the dark on a top step that isn't there. But it could not be true. It was true; the place in the desk was empty. Everything changed. In the tight strangeness my father and mother were not like them; I did not feel like me.

They asked, Had I told someone? No. Had I never said anything to anyone, ever, about that money? No. Had I seen a stranger near the wagon when they were not there? No. Or in camp? No.

My mother said it wasn't possible; not the Cooleys. My father agreed, no, not them. It must be there. My mother had seen it last in Kansas.

They took every sheet of writing paper out of the desk and shook it; they took each letter out of its envelope, unfolded it, looked into the empty envelope. They turned the desk upside down and shook it, the felt-covered inside lids flapping. My mother said they were losing their senses. Suddenly she thought, hoped, asked, Had I taken it myself, to play with?

NO! I felt scalded. She asked, Was I sure? I hadn't just opened the desk sometime, for fun? My throat swelled shut; I shook my head, no. "Don't cry," she said automatically. I wouldn't cry, I never cried, I was angry, insulted, miserable, I was not a

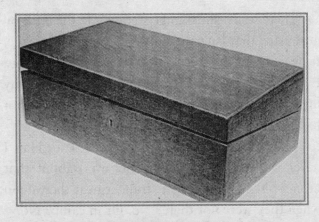

BOTH: COMSTOCK & SONS, SPRINGFIELD, MISSOURI

Two views of the lap desk that held the $100 bill.

baby who'd play with money or open that desk for fun, I was going on eight years old. I was little, alone, and scared. My father and mother sat there, still. In the long stillness I sank slowly into nothing but terror, pure terror without cause or object, a nightmare terror.

Finally my mother said, "Well." She meant, No use crying over spilled milk. What can't be cured must be endured. My father told her not to blame herself, it wasn't her fault. Carefully she peeled off her thin kid gloves. She turned them right-side-out finger by finger, smoothed them. She said that he'd better go explain to the banker.

Somehow the worst was over when he tried to put it off, saying something might turn up, and she flared out that he knew as well as she did, "nothing turns up that we don't turn up ourselves." Then she told me to run away and play, and I remembered the unwashed dishes. She had forgotten them.

For days, I don't remember how many days, everything was the same as ever and not at all the same. I said nothing about the disaster; I didn't want to. My mother told Mrs. Cooley that they thought best to take time to make up their minds. My father looked for work in town. My mother knew nobody there. Mr. Cooley sold one of his teams and one wagon; and Paul and George were going to move into the hotel and help run it. I knew we could sell the horses, but what then? Covered wagons were going by every day, going both ways as usual, some camping overnight nearby. Often I tried to think what would happen when we had nothing to eat; I couldn't.

Blackberries were fewer now and smaller. I was deep in the briary patch, hunting them, when my mother called, and called again before I could get out without tearing my dress on the clutching thorns and run over the sharp stones to the camp. My father was hitching up, my mother was putting last things into the wagon. They had bought the farm. She had found the hundred dollar bill. In the writing desk. The jolting had slipped it into a crack in the desk and I was to stop asking questions and get into the wagon. Just as she was, my mother had found my father and gone to sign the papers, and just as I was, without even washing my feet, I was to obey her and get up onto that wagon seat, *now*, and no more words about it.

The town began with two small houses on a side road in the woods. Then there were two big houses in large yards with trees, and a cunning little low house right at the edge of the gravel sidewalk. On the other side of the road, opposite the little house, stairs went up the side of the hotel where Paul and George would live. In front of the hotel was the Square, with trees in it and lines of hitching posts around it, except on the far side where the railroad track was. We were driving along Main Street, and it was on one side of us and in front of us and behind us, too; it went around three sides of the Square. It was three solid rows of stores behind three high board sidewalks. This was The Gem City of the Ozarks.

We passed a big Reynolds General Store, with two large windows full of things, the door between them. Men were loafing, whittling, talking and spitting along the high board walk. There were small stores, The Bank of Mansfield, a Boston Racket store with "Opera House" painted on the windows upstairs, Hoover's Livery Stable and horses in a feed lot, then another big house inside a wire fence. Past a blacksmith shop the dusty road went downhill to cross a little bridge. The long hillside was orchard and pasture, but houses began where the road went up again beyond the bridge. In all there must have been a dozen houses, in fenced yards with gates, behind paths through the weeds on both sides of the road.

All the houses had front porches; all were painted and trimmed with different colors and wooden lace. Behind them were vegetable gardens and clotheslines, barns and chicken houses; some had pigpens. Two had an upstairs; one of these had a bay window and a cupola. Behind the houses on our right was the railroad enbankment; behind those on the left, two more houses and a high grassy hill against the sky.

At the top of the road's long climb stood the schoolhouse where I would go to school. It stood square, two stories high, with windows all around, and its bell tower up above the double doors. All beyond it was woods; it was in the edge of the woods but not a single stump remained on the ground trodden bare and hard about it. There was a well beside it; behind it a woodshed and two privies: Boys and Girls.

I looked as long as I could, but the road turned away from the schoolhouse to follow the railroad track. The wheel tracks went beside the iron rails with a row of poles holding a telegraph wire on glass knobs above them. There were two houses in the woods; then the road turned into the woods and left the railroad behind us.

Now there was nothing but woods on either side, and the two wheel tracks went straight and slowly downward. Between them were stumps and big rocks. The wagon jolted and lurched over rocks in the dust and the horses' iron shoes clattered on them.

From the talk over my head I learned how lucky it was that the last cent had been just enough to pay for the salt pork and cornmeal. We could make out all right now, selling wood, and do well when the apple trees were in bearing. Paying off the mortgage would be easy then. Three hundred dollars at twelve percent, pounded every three months. (Why would they be pounded? I wondered.) My mother could do the arithmetic in her head. They ought to be able to carry it if they kept their health.

Either then or later I learned from such talk that some very foolish man had bought all those little apple trees from a smart salesman though he had no cleared land. When they came in their bundles, he had no clearing to set them out in; but he had signed papers, so he had to mortgage the land to pay for them. Then he just gave up. Between two days, he left the land and the cabin, the little apple trees root-buried in a trench, and the mortgage. So my father and mother got them from the banker.

The road went up again, it seemed to go almost vertically up a long, long hill but my father turned the horses away from it, onto a fainter track in a valley. Beside us now a stream of water as clear as glass ran over flat ledges and through shadow pools. In a little while the wagon tracks turned to ford a pool. The horses stopped to drink and my mother said, "Here we are!" She asked me what I thought of it, but I saw nothing to think about. The creek came from our own spring, she told me. Across the creek the woods went up a low hill in the yellow light of the sinking sun; the wheel tracks went on down the curve of the creek, and trees hid them.

My father drove up the hill through the woods. The horses climbed clumsily, the flat rocks slipping under their feet. At the top of the hill we came into a tiny clearing at the edge of a deep ravine, and there stood a little log house.

Quick as a squirrel, I was down over the wheel and around the corner of logs' ends. A rough, thick door stood open; I was in the house, I was in a narrow little room, its floor of earth and dead leaves, but beyond a doorway was a larger room that had a wooden floor. This room was bare and

Rocky Ridge Farm in Mansfield after Almanzo had cleared a good deal of the land. Laura probably took this photograph about 1910.   R.W.L.

clean, it smelled like the woods, dead leaves were blown into its corners. There was a big fireplace and sure enough, as that woman had said, no windows. There was a square hole in the wall of peeled logs; an empty hole, but it had a rough wooden door hanging open, like the house door.

Nothing more was to be seen there. But I hadn't noticed that in the narrow room the logs of the wall around the door were papered with newspapers. Large black letters in curleycues stopped me; I stood and read: "Carter's Little Liver Pills," and a philosophical question which I kept trying and failing to answer for so long afterward that I have never forgotten it: What is life without a liver?

That problem was too much for me; for the moment, I postponed the struggle with it. Outside, some chunks of bark had fallen from the house wall, and between all the logs was yellow clay, dry and hard and cracked to bits. Not far away the path from the door went down, steeper than stairs, into the ravine. As usual, my mother called to me to be careful.

The ravine was shadowy, darker in its narrow bottom. It ended in one huge rock as big as a big house. Behind the rock was a hollow sound of running water, and water ran from beneath it into a little pool as round as a washtub and half as deep. Ferns hung over the darling pool, and from a bough above it dangled a hollowed-out gourd for dipping up the water.

I drank a delicious cold gourdful, looking up and up the mountainside above the spring. It was all dark woods, only the very tips of the highest trees in sudden yellow light. All down the dark ravine the water chuckled eerily. Something moved stealthily in the leaves under the bushes. I clambered up the path as fast as I could.

The cabin we lived in during the first winter in Mansfield.
It was part of the barn when this picture was taken. The
horses are the team which brought us down from Dakota.
My father is sitting in a buggy for which he traded the
hack, when we were rich enough to have a wagon and
a buggy.   R.W.L.

This photo of Laura was taken in the ravine just below
the spring.

LAURA INGALLS WILDER HOME ASSOCIATION

A neighbor's cabin. My father is pictured by it in his "buffalo coat," which was made from the skin of a buffalo killed in Dakota. R.W.L.

The horses were unhitched and picketed, the hens in their coop on the ground. My father and mother were taking out things over the wagon's opened endgate. We would eat supper outdoors and sleep one more night in the wagon. My mother meant to scrub that cabin floor from top to bottom before we moved into it. We could still see well enough in the shadowy daylight, but inside the wagon it was too dark to find things. My father rummaged for the lantern.

He pressed the spring that lifted its thick glass globe, he touched the match-flame to the wick and carefully lowered the globe into its place, and suddenly the lantern was shining in darkness. He held it up, looking for a place to hang it, and there in the edge of its light stood a strange man.

The man's feet were bare, his pants were patched over patches and torn. He was tall, thin, bony, and his eyes glittered from a bush of hair and whiskers. He came a step nearer and quick as a snake my mother's hand slid into the pocket where her revolver was. She waited, ready. Slowly my father said, "Hello there."

The man said he wanted work, he was looking for a chance to work for something to eat. My father answered that we were just moving in, as he could see; we didn't have work to give anybody. Too bad, but maybe better luck in town, just over the next hill, not much more than a mile to the west.

"You got a good place here," the man said. He was bony, but big. After a minute my father said it would be a good place someday, he guessed. Then we all stood silent as if we couldn't move.

The man began to talk quietly, slowly, almost dreamily. They had to get something to eat, he said. His wife and five children were down in the wagon by the creek. They had been traveling all summer looking for work. They could not go on any longer. This was the third day they'd had nothing to eat. He had to get work so he came up the wagon tracks—they couldn't go on without something to eat.

He stopped, there was nothing more to say. Nothing to do. Now I knew what happened when you had nothing to eat. What happens is, nothing.

Suddenly, my father was talking and moving quickly, not deliberate at all. He said he needed help making wood, provided the man would come help him tomorrow, he'd divide what little— He was reaching into the wagon. At sight of the slab of salted fat pork my mother cried out, "Manly, *no! We've got Rose.*" He paid no attention. The butcher knife in his hand cut through the white meat. He opened a corner of the sack and poured cornmeal into the little tin pail. He was asking, did the man have a good ax? He said they'd start early, at sun-up, put in a good day's work and if the wood sold he'd treat the man right. Bring an ax if he had one. Be sure to bring back the pail. That's all right, don't mention it, see you tomorrow.

The man was gone into the darkness. He had not said a word. Afterward my mother always said that she expected never to see that vagabond again, nor her tin pail, either. At the time she said nothing. My father made the fire under the camp stove and she cooked supper. We had fried salt pork and corn-dodgers, and slept in the wagon.

The man woke us in the false dawn, bringing the tin pail and his ax. He was a better woodsman than my father. All that day while my mother and I cleaned the house and lugged things from the wagon to put on the dry, scrubbed floor, they worked in the woods. They worked as long as they could see. Then my mother held the lantern and they took the top and curtains off the wagon, and stacked up high in it all the stove wood that it would hold.

Early next morning my father set out to sell the

wood in town. The man worked with a will while he was gone. He was gone all day. At night he had not come. The strange man went down the hill, my mother lit the lamp, turned low to save the kerosene. Still it was some time before we heard the wagon jolting. My mother lit the lantern, then said I'd better take it to him.

I rushed out with it. The wagon box was empty and I almost shouted, "You sold it!"

"Finally I did," my father said in triumph.

"How much did you get for it?" I asked. He was beginning to unharness the horses. He bragged, "Fifty cents."

I set down the lantern and ran into the house to tell my mother, "Fifty cents! He sold it all for fifty cents!" Her whole face trembled and seemed to melt into softness, she sighed a long sigh. "Aren't you glad?" I exulted.

"Glad? Of course I'm glad!" she snapped at me and to herself, "Oh, thanks be!"

I ran out again, I pranced out, to tell my father how glad she was. And he said, with a sound of crying in his voice, "Oh, why did you tell her? I wanted to surprise her."

You do such things, little things, horrible, cruel, without thinking, not meaning to. You have done it; nothing can undo it. This is a thing you can never forget.

How long that man worked with my father I don't remember. I cannot remember his name nor anything at all about his family camping down by the creek. Surely I knew those children; they must have been there for weeks. I remember that he and my father were roofing the little log barn, the day I chased the rabbit.

The leaves had fallen from all the trees but the oaks then, and the oaks wore their winter red that day. There was light snow or frost underfoot, so cold that it burned my bare feet, and my breath puffed white in the air. I chased that rabbit over the hills, up and down and back again until, exhausted, it hid in a hollow log; I stopped up the log's ends with rocks and fetched both men from their work on the roof to chop out the rabbit and kill it.

The day was Saturday; I was going to school then. For Sunday dinner we had rabbit stew, with gravy on mashed potatoes and on our cornbread. And on Monday I found in my lunch-pail at school one of that rabbit's legs; my mother had saved it and packed it with the cornbread in the little tin pail, to surprise me.

The man and his family must have gone on

west or south, early that winter. He must have earned provisions for the trip. I remember walking to school through the snowy woods in my shoes and stockings, hearing the thuds of my father's ax sounding fainter as I went; and coming home with the sunset red behind me to hear the whirr-whirr of the crosscut saw growing sharper in the frosty air. The ax was too heavy for my mother; my father would not trust her with its sharpness, but she could safely handle one end of the crosscut saw.

Winter evenings were cozy in the cabin. The horses were warm in the little barn, the hens in the new wooden coop. Snow banked against the log walls and long icicles hung from the eaves. A good fire of hickory logs burned in the fireplace. In its heat, over a newspaper spread on the hearth, my father worked oil into the harness-straps between his oily-black hands. I sat on the floor, carefully building a house of corncobs, and my mother sat by the table, knitting needles flashing while she knitted warm woolen socks for my father and read to us from a book propped under the kerosene lamp. She read us Tennyson's poems and Scott's poems; those books were ours. And she read us Prescott's *Conquest of Mexico*, and

Conquest of Peru, and *The Green Mountain Boys*, and *John Halifax, Gentleman*. She read us *The Leatherstocking Tales*, and another true book, the biggest of all: *Ancient, Medieval and Modern History*. I borrowed those from the shelf of lending-books in the Fourth Reader room at school. The teachers let me borrow them, though I wasn't in Fourth Reader yet.

I remember the Sunday afternoon when my father and mother planned the new house. We had got the cow that spring; I must have been ten years old, going on eleven. On Sunday afternoons in warm weather, when company wasn't spending the day with us or we were not spending it in town with the Cooleys, my father and mother in their Sunday clothes went walking sedately over the land while I, in mine, minded the cabin. They had cleared twenty acres and set out all the little apple trees, and we had the cow, that Sunday afternoon when they decided where to build the house.

From my swing in the oak tree by the cabin, Fido and I saw them standing and talking under the huge old white-oak tree not far away. They talked a long while. Then my father went to lead the cow to water and change her picket-peg, and my mother called me to see the spot where our

Part of Rocky Ridge Farm as it looked in 1962.

house would be.

It would be under the great old white-oak at the edge of the hill where we stood. Here the ground sloped more gently down into the ravine and rose steeply up the wooded mountain to the south. You could see the brook running from the widening mouth of the ravine and curving to the north and east around the base of the rounded hill. You could hear the water rippling over the limestone ledges. It was springtime; the hickory trees on the hill were in young green leaves, the oak leaves were pink, and all the flinty ground beneath them was covered with one blue-purple mat of dog's-tooth violets. Along the brook the service trees were blooming misty white. The ancient white-oak was lively with dozens of young squirrels whisking into and out of their nests in the hollow branches.

My mother stood under it in her brown-sprigged white lawn dress, her long braid hanging down her back. Below the curled bangs her eyes were as purple-blue as the violets. It would be a white house, she said, all built from our farm. Everything we needed to build it was on the land: good oak beams and boards, stones for the foundation and the fireplace. The house would have

large windows looking west across the brook, over
the gentle little valley and up the wooded hills that
hid the town, to the sunset colors in the sky. There
would be a nice big porch to the north, cool on hot
summer afternoons. The kitchen would be big
enough to hold a wood stove for winter and one of
the new kerosene stoves that wouldn't heat up the
place worse in summer. Every window would be
screened with mosquito netting. There would be a
well, with a pump, just outside the kitchen door;
no more lugging water from the spring. And in the
parlor there would be a bookcase, no, *two* bookcases, big bookcases full of books, and a hanging
lamp to read them by, on winter evenings by the
fireplace.

When the mortgage is paid, in only a few more
years, she said, and when the orchard is in bearing,
if prices are good then, we will fence the whole
place with wire and build the barn bigger; we will
have more stock by then. And after that, we can
begin to build the house.

She woke from the dream with a start and a
Goodness! it's chore-time! I'd better take the milk
pail to my father, she said, and feed the hens before
they went to roost; don't forget to fill their water

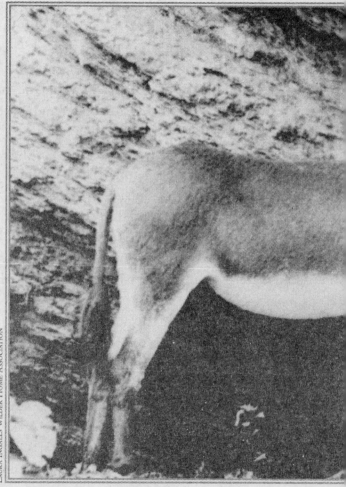

When I was a little girl in the Ozarks, I had a donkey whose name was Spookendyke.   R.W.L.

Laura's dream realized: the house that she and Almanzo built of materials from the farm. The wellhouse is outside the kitchen door. The home is now preserved as a memorial museum by the Laura Ingalls Wilder Home Association of Mansfield, Missouri. R.W.L.

pans, and bring in the eggs; be careful not to break one. Oh, now that we had the cow, we'd have a treat for Sunday supper, French toast with that wild honey, to surprise my father. How wonderful it was to have a cow again.

While I scattered corn for the hens, fetched water from the spring to fill their pans, and hunted for eggs that the broody hens hid in the haymow, in the straw stack, and even in the wild grasses, I heard her whistling in the cabin, getting supper.

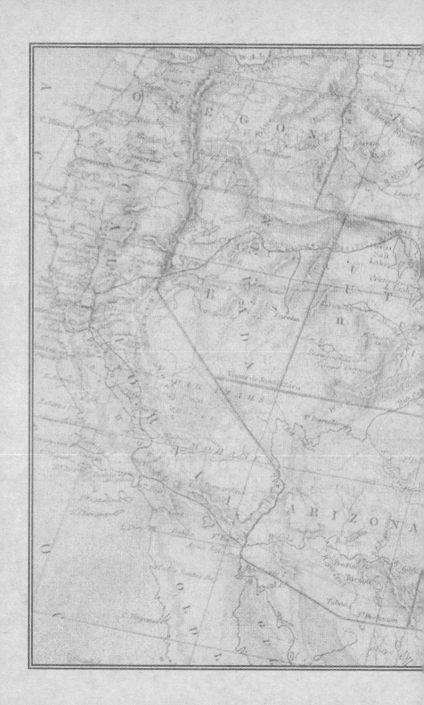

Part Two

WEST FROM HOME

Letters of
Laura Ingalls Wilder
San Francisco, 1915

Edited by Roger Lea MacBride

Roger Lea MacBride thanks each person who helped make this trip come alive:

Irene Lichty, late curator of the Laura Ingalls Wilder–Rose Wilder Lane Museum in Mansfield, Missouri; *Elizabeth Anderson*, who at the time this book was written was with the University of Missouri Library in Columbia; *Evelyn Wells*, biographer of Fremont Older; and the late *Rose Bunch*, whom Roger met in her apartment one floor above Rose's.

For the photographs: the marvelous *Raymond Moulin*, who as the young son of photographer Gabriel saw the fair; *Gladys Hansen* of Special Collections of the San Francisco Public Library; *Larry Leiurance* and *Rene Casenave* of the San Francisco *Examiner*; and the *J. Nielson Rogers* family.

This photograph of Laura Ingalls Wilder was taken about two years after her stay in San Francisco.

Almanzo Wilder, in the field of Rocky Ridge, 1908.

Introduction

Tumbled in a cardboard box along with old recipes, faded pictures, and newspaper clippings of persons and events long gone, I found these letters and postcards from Laura Ingalls Wilder to her husband, Almanzo. The first few were addressed in pencil to Mr. A. J. Wilder, Mansfield, Missouri, on envelopes with the two-cent first-class stamp imprinted upon them by the U.S. Post Office. The later ones were mostly in envelopes bearing the return address "The *Bulletin*, San Francisco," addressed by typewriter, and personally stamped.

Laura was always frugal. The writing paper she used was inexpensive and unlined. It wouldn't take

Rose Wilder Lane, a year or so after Laura's visit to San Francisco.

ink, so she used her soft pencil. In San Francisco she sometimes typed on the cheap yellow typewriter paper used by her daughter Rose as a newspaper reporter. The whole bundle of letters was tied with a short length of thin white grocery-store string that had sawn through the crumbling edges of the envelopes over the years. Either Manly or Laura had put them all together in a safe place for looking at in years to come.

After Laura's death in 1957, Rose in her grief sifted through her mother's papers and tossed into cartons those things that she thought she might want to look at later. But she was never able to bring herself to do so. Then, when Rose died in 1968, I, as her friend and executor, had the task of going through her papers. I had much the same feeling, and it wasn't until a few years later that I really wanted to read those things that I had set aside. It was then that I opened the carton.

As readers of her Little House books know, Laura was a pioneer girl who traveled throughout the Midwest during her childhood. She married Almanzo in 1885 and they homesteaded near De Smet, Dakota Territory. Storms, fire, plagues of locusts, and drought finally forced them to seek a new start in Mansfield, Missouri—"The Land of the Big Red Apple," as its promoters called it.

Life on the new farm was a hard scrabble. During the early years the land couldn't support the small family, so Almanzo took a job selling kerosene for the Waters Pierce Oil Company. Laura managed customer billing and accounts payable, to free Almanzo to do whatever work was necessary at the farm. Eventually, the farm began to prosper and their lives became increasingly happy. Their only child, Rose, recalled the scene later:

*At night I took a book home from school,
and after supper Papa would pop a big pan
of popcorn and Mama Bess [Laura, whose
middle name was Elizabeth, was called that
within her family to avoid confusion with
Almanzo's sister Laura] would read aloud
while he and I ate it. She sat beside the table
with the lamp on it. Her hair was combed
back smoothly and braided in a heavy braid
and the lamplight glistened on it.*

*Papa sat on the other side of the table, the
pan of popcorn between his knees, and ate
slowly and methodically, kernel by kernel.
He liked to look at the shape of each one;
he often remarked that no two were alike
and yet they were all pretty. It was the cozy,
comfortable hour for all of us. We had had
supper, the room was warm, we were alone
together, the horses fed and sleeping in the
barn, nothing to worry us till tomorrow, and
Mama Bess was reading. That was best of all.*

Rose's success in later life—she was a world-
famous author before her mother was known outside the Ozarks—was in no small part testimony
to the character and intelligence of her parents.

She went to work first as a telegrapher for Western Union, then as one of the first real estate saleswomen in California, and in 1914 was a feature writer for the San Francisco *Bulletin* under the tutelage of that great American editor Fremont Older.

By this time she was married, brimful of early success, and eager to share her joys with her mother. She had previously urged her mother to come west to San Francisco, but the plans had not materialized.

Now, in 1915, the great World's Fair, called the Panama-Pacific International Exposition, was scheduled to open in San Francisco to celebrate the completion of the magnificent canal through Panama. This was to be a splendid spectacle to show the world that California had truly come into its own in every way.

Rose was eager to have her mother come out to visit her in this, of all years. Rose's letter inviting her mother is undated, and to settle details there must have been correspondence, since lost, between that and Laura's first letter. One problem was having both Laura and Manly leave the farm—someone had to stay home to run it. Generous to a fault as always, and perhaps at heart

127

more of a farmer and less of a traveler than Laura, Manly insisted that she go, and she did. But not without promising that she would be Manly's eyes across the western United States and at the Fair, much as she had been the eyes for her sister, Mary, in her childhood.

Thanks to that arrangement we can almost go back in time to an era that would otherwise be forever veiled to most of us. We share a transcontinental train trip with the pioneer girl who first crossed the plains in a covered wagon; we savor her reactions to the likes of Henry Ford and Charlie Chaplin, and we marvel with her at the ocean, San Francisco's Chinatown, aerial acrobatics, and above all the great Fair.

The sun is shining again in the summer of 1915, and here they are: Laura just turned forty-eight, and her twenty-nine-year-old daughter, in an adventure for them and for us.

Roger Lea MacBride, 1974

On the Way

*In the spring of 1915 Laura's only daughter
Rose wrote to her on the stationery of the
newspaper for which she was a reporter.*

The *Bulletin*
San Francisco, Calif.

Mrs. A. J. Wilder
Rocky Ridge Farm
Mansfield, Missouri

Dearest Mama Bess—

I simply can't stand being so homesick for you
any more.

You must plan to come out here in July or, at
latest, August. You've simply GOT to, so let me

hear no argument about it. I know how you felt about being disappointed before, because I felt every bit as bad, I guess badder, because I was terribly disappointed for myself and twice as disappointed for you, and sore besides because I could not manage better. But this time I am quite sure it can be managed. Unless something very catastrophic happens, like war, or another earthquake, or something.

It won't be as I planned to have you out, because we haven't the machine [automobile] now, and both Gillette [Rose's husband] and I are working, and there isn't so awfully much money. But we can have a pleasant time together, anyway. You can see San Francisco and the Fair, and meet my friends, and we can play together all the time that I'm not working. I have worked this job into a sort of movable feast, so that I don't have to be in the office any regular hours, and you can go with me on lots of my outside work—I can arrange for you to have an aeroplane flight* if you like, and we can eat in all the little interesting restaurants.

*Rose had by then flown over San Francisco Bay strapped to the wing of Lincoln Beachey's plane—the same Beachey who was killed very early during the 1915 Exposition. He was the first American to loop the loop. Young Art Smith was his replacement

I have it figured out that sometime in July I will be able to send you the fare, and while you are here and maybe right along afterward I can send you $5 a week to make up for what you will lose in chickens, etc., by the trip.† I should think by that time all the little ones would be out of the way, and there wouldn't be so much work with them. The strawberries will be gone, and the pressure of work won't be so bad. You will miss most of the very hot weather, too.

I think by getting away from it all for awhile, and playing around with a bunch of people who are writing and drawing and otherwise being near-artists, you will get an entirely new viewpoint on things there, and be able to see a lot of new things to write when you go back. If the farm-paper market is closed, there are scads of other markets open. I got an invitation to submit stories to an eastern magazine the other day which I could turn over to you. I haven't time to write for it myself—it is only a little magazine, but would probably pay

at the Fair. A photo of Smith looping, while trailing smoke to thrill the crowd, is on page 162.

†To make up for the financial drain of Laura's not being at the farm.

$50 or so for a story. When you get things to running so that the farm work won't take up so much time you can do things like that. And with the notes and mortagages paid off and your lovely home all built, you and Papa can take things easier. Next year you can maybe get off and make a little trip together to Louisiana or someplace. The way it looks to me, there are only the debts to clear off and you will have a self-supporting home and can use the little extra sums—the bunches of money, like from the apples or strawberries—that come in, to play with.

Anyway, please plan to come out here in July or August, and get the work in shape so you can leave it for three months.

Don't get any new clothes, because we can get those here, except underwear. Suits and things are as cheap here as there, and perhaps the styles would be different—we can get things in a few days from the shops, and then when you go back your things will all be new to the people there. Bring warm things, because it will be cool here—you will wear a suit all the time except in the evening, and probably most of the time then—we don't dress up in the evening except on a rare occasion like a box-party, or something. I have a wonderful dressmaker, who can whip things into shape and astonish you, so don't bother making over anything, just bring it along. I was thinking maybe your rose silk would be pretty with a black lace over it and some coral beads. If you get anything, get some shoes and slippers from Sears Roebuck—they cost out of sight here. Don't bring any extra hats, because by July everyone here will be wearing fall hats and we can get one here. Bring your furs and warm underwear and gloves and shoes, that's all.

I will not talk much about what we will do, because then you will be disappointed when you get here. But we can visit, and play around in Chinatown together some, and you can meet the people I know. And you can get acquainted with San Francisco. I am glad you are from the Ozarks, because everything is hills here. It will be foggy and windy and dusty and gray and you will not like San Francisco while you are here, and then when you go away you will always want to come back. 'Tis ever thus. If you like you shall eat an octopus. I promise that.

What do you think of the Art Smith story? It is going fairly well. What do you think of the "Confessions of a Physician"? I think it is awful rot, myself, but the whole *Bulletin* staff thinks it is splendid stuff. I don't know that anyone else does. I will probably be back on the staff of Bessie's* [women's] page sometime in June. I don't mind, it is a soft snap. I will write her another story and loaf all the time.

With much love,
Rose

—᠁—

And so Laura set out. She couldn't wait to start describing what she saw and did for her husband, Almanzo. This letter was written during her first stop, at a friend's house only sixty miles from home.

Springfield, Mo.
Saturday P.M.
August 21, 1915

Manly Dear,

I am resting in Mabel's room for two hours while she goes to one of her customers' houses and gives them a beautifying treatment. Then she is going with me to get my hat. I nearly got "licked before I started" this morning [from Mansfield].

*Bessie Beatty, who had earlier launched Rose's career by persuading her to do some freelance stories for the *Bulletin*.

They said the train would be half an hour late so I went over to Youngs' and Mrs. Y. gave me a cup of coffee—train ran in in just ten minutes. I ran from Youngs' and around the train and caught it, though it had to wait while John brought my suitcase and package from the office.

I will have to go on without my glasses. Had my eyes examined this morning and the oculist said it would take three or four days to make them to fit my eyes. He said, and seemed to prove it with his apparatus, that my left eye is doing all the work and my right eye is pretty poor. He said my left eye was normal, that is as it should be, but it was a bad strain on it to work alone, but the sight of my right eye was all wrong. He says the glasses I should have will have to be specially prepared and that I should wear them all the time to save my eyes, instead of wearing them just when I read, and oh dear me, he says they will cost me $20.

If [Dr.] Fuson is in town I'm going up to see him and find out if these people are all right or if they are on the beat and then I'll know better what to do. I told him I could not wait for the glasses as I was going to California, but if he would keep the record I would see about them when I came back. He said he would do that and if I find I can do no better I can write him and he will send them to me when I come home.

How are you and Inky [their dog] I wonder? The country here is awfully washed. We did not get it all. Was the lettuce seed ruined? Perhaps you'd better look.

Take good care of yourself and Inky and I'll come back before you get to learn how to get on without me. Mabel and I are going out this afternoon and she will see me on the Kansas City train at 10:40 this evening.

With love,
Bessie

—— ✺ ——

Kansas City
Sunday, August 22, 1915

Manly Dear,

I just did make my train. Train from Springfield was two hours late, loaded with people trying to get to St. Louis from the south and having to come around by Kansas City. There were fifteen coaches and two engines on the train. I sat all the way with a St. Louis German who smelled of beer and said V instead of W, but he was very kind and treated me to peaches and in the night it got cold and he woke me up, laying his extra coat very softly over me. He was old and gray-headed and a perfect gentleman. I'm going to find everyone kind and all the help I need, as usual. Hope you and Inky are all right.

Love to you both,
Bessie

Monday morning, 7 A.M.
August 23, 1915

Manly Dear,

Write me so I'll know how everything is when I first get there. Do you remember the address: Mrs. Gillette Lane, c/o The *Bulletin*, San Francisco, California.

We should be in Denver but we are 198 miles away. Four hours and fifteen minutes late, but trying our best to make up the time. There was a washout last night 400 feet long and 40 feet wide, and while I slept soundly on the safe side someone must have worked like the mischief fixing it so we could cross over. It is queer-looking country, great hills of sand with the grass so thin over it that the sand shows through. Sand cliffs along the river and clumps of willows and cottonwoods along the river but not a tree anywhere else, just the sand hills rolling across in every direction. It must be the big ranch country. Every once in a while there will be a house and a barn and a windmill with corrals near. I can see bunches of horses and cattle farther away and bunches of calves nearer the barns. I counted fifty little calves in one bunch and there have been larger ones.

All yesterday there was only one other woman in the car and she had her berth made up and stayed in it. There were three men. I asked one of them if he knew just where we were and so we got to talking. He is a full-blooded Frenchman and his home is Baltimore, Maryland.

Saw my first sage brush this morning. A dwarf variety. It is in little clumps all over the prairie.

I just saw so many, many cattle—must have been 200 in a big pasture. The range is fenced up, you know. The land is so *flat*. This lawyer from Nebraska says it is *beautiful* and the old Frenchman and I smile at each other. He thinks it looks like a great country but not pretty. I don't like the lawyer chap even if he is a graduate of Harvard as he says. He talks too much with his mouth and takes much for granted. Sat down in the seat with me without being asked. I've frozen him out and my Frenchman has shook him and is talking with a nice boy about the trip out of Denver. The Frenchman is on his way to San Francisco but stops over at Denver, while I go on. He was in Belgium just before the war and saw the Cathedral of Rheims, the one the Germans destroyed, you know, and that famous stained rose window that can never be replaced. He is about 75 years old and has told me of his wife who is a New Orleans Frenchwoman, and his mother who made several trips from New Orleans to Europe in sailing vessels when she was a girl.

The hills have rock tops now and are awfully funny-looking. —I was interrupted here by [a man who] was a cowboy in Nebraska when he was young but is now a lawyer. He is on his way to Snake River Valley in Wyoming where he has a ranch.

The country is growing smooth again. We are past the funny hills. We are in Colorado now. There is homestead land here and rights can be bought where it is already taken for from $350 to

$500 for 320 acres.* The homesteads here are 320 instead of 160, a new law. It is dry farming or irrigation, as one prefers. A lake of underground water furnishes irrigation if pumped. The country is flat and I can see as far as my eyes will let me. We will be in Denver about noon and I am told I can get [a train] out at three o'clock. I have already missed the train I expected to take. Turned my watch back an hour. Western time now.

—⁓—

Denver
Monday noon

Well I missed connections at Denver and am at a hotel near the depot. I can go out at seven o'clock tonight and miss seeing the scenery. I hate to do it but rather think I will. If not I can start from here at eight in the morning. I'm rather tired and I wish I was through with the trip. So far everything out of the car windows has been ugly since I left the Ozarks.

I do wish I knew how you and Inky were getting along and if Mr. Nall [a hired hand] came. I'm

*Instead of following the rules of the Homestead Act themselves, people could also purchase land from individuals who had acquired property by going that route.

so aggravated about that washout that threw the train late but then I suppose a wait is better than an accident.

Oh, Dr. Fuson said to get me a pair of glasses for a dollar that would magnify so I could read while I'm away and when I come back he'll take me to the oculist that does his work and have him fix my eyes up right. He says those folks are a fraud and Mabel said she thought they were on the beat.

Love to you and Inky,

Bessie

Denver, Monday P.M.
August 23, 1915

Manly Dear,

Well, I decided to stay over. I figured it out this way. Rose routed me this way so I could see this part of the country and I might never come this way again. If I had gone on tonight I would have had to take a berth and instead I will pay less for my night's rest here. I am undressed and in my room and I have had a cup of hot tea and some hot toast at half past two so I will not go down again. I'm going to bed and sleep the rest of the afternoon and tonight, and go on fresh in the morning. I will have some sleep ahead and will not take a berth tomorrow, so I will save the amount of my hotel bill here and it will be fun for one day to ride in the common coach and see the people. One travels with their own crowd in a Pullman and does not get a chance to see the people of the country they are going through. So I have figured that by what I save in this way it will cost no more to stay over here, and then I will see the country Rose planned for me to see and get to Frisco the time of day she planned for me to arrive if nothing else happens to prevent.

The country stayed flat-looking clear to Denver but I could tell by the air that we were up high and the engine seemed to be climbing. A man told me that we are just one mile above sea level but the country stayed, as to looks, just as I wrote you in my letter on the train.

They were cutting wheat and threshing, hauling in from the shocks. I saw some irrigating ditches and some fields of potatoes, and the Columbia River runs among grass banks and looks a good deal like the Missouri, only not quite so muddy. The grass grows so thin on the ground that I could see the dirt through it all the way.

My nice Frenchman, Victor Brun, helped me

over to the hotel and after I had been in my room awhile he called me to know if I was resting well and if there was anything he could do for me outside. He is very eager to help me and very much afraid he will presume. He went out sight-seeing so I'll likely not see him again. When I go in the morning I'm going to leave a note with the clerk asking him to Rocky Ridge. He is traveling a good deal now. Says he decided he wanted to see a little of the world before he died. And he might come who knows. I'm sure you would like him. Remember, if you can, to ask me to tell you what he told me about Maryland. I will have so much to tell you I'm afraid I'll forget and it is very interesting. I'm going to sleep now and will mail this in the morning.

Hurried away from the hotel so fast this morning I forgot to mail this. Am safely on board train for Ogden, and have the first glimpse of the mountains. Conductor coming, I'll give him this.*

Bessie

—⁓—

*The envelope containing this letter was postmarked Malta, Colorado.

On the train
from Denver to Salt Lake
August 25, 1915

Manly Dear,

I wish you were here. Half the fun I lose because I am all the time wishing for you.

We passed through the most desolate country this morning—the first desert I've seen. The mountains were around the edges and as the sun rose they showed the most beautiful soft colors. There were miles and miles and miles of sand dunes without a spear of grass or a green thing, only now and then where there was a tiny ranch and a ditch of water from the river. We are climbing up out of the desert now through the encircling rim of mountains. They are simply frightful. Huge masses and ramparts of rock, just bare rock in every fantastic shape imaginable. They are not like I thought. I had supposed there were forests among the rocky peaks, but there is only once in a great ways a stunted pine. The mountains look like those pictures of old castles in Austria we were looking at, and such wonderful fortified places they would make—such castles could be made on them!

I'll have to wait three hours in Salt Lake—then

a ride of an hour to Ogden and there is my last change. Then it is a straightway for San Francisco. The cars are a perfect jam, so overcrowded no one can be comfortable. No sleeper to be had and I'm awfully tired. If I had known what a hard trip it would be I don't believe I'd have had the courage, but still I'm sure I'll always be glad I came. If I make connections I ought to be in San Francisco tomorrow, but the train is late and I do not know how it will be. There will be one more ugly night anyway.

Well, yesterday the acquaintances I made were an Englishman and his family. They live in Ogden and were down to Denver on a trip. He worked in the cotton mills in England when he was seven and until he was grown. He had been a Bryan Democrat* but is changing to a Socialist, and the woman votes.†

We are going through tunnel after tunnel.

I saw in yesterday's paper that the Russian fleet the Germans had penned up in the Baltic had sunk eleven German warships with the loss of only one Russian.

---

*A supporter of William Jennings Bryan, the secretary of state.
†There was female suffrage in Ogden, Utah, in 1915.

I wish I knew how you and Inky were getting along and if Mr. Nall was with you. Hope to hear soon after I get to Frisco. I am too tired to write interestingly so I'll quit.

With love,
Bessie

———⟊———

POSTCARD

Salt Lake City
August 25, 1915

Train leaves Salt Lake 5:30—San Francisco train waits for us at Ogden so I'm all right. San Francisco tomorrow.

Bessie

———⟊———

Waiting in the depot in
Salt Lake City
August 25, 1915

Manly Dear,

This is the unhandiest depot I ever saw. I can't buy or reserve a Pullman ticket in the building. Have to go to some number on some street out in the town so I'm letting it go. I'd have to check my baggage and hire a boy to take me to the place, and there is not a red cap in sight. It is 1:15 and my train does not go to Ogden until 5:30 so I'm going to sit here and take notice. Goodness knows how I'll find things at Ogden when I get there at 6:30. I'll likely have to stay all night but it will be the last change, and never again for me. When I go anywhere on the train I'll go the quickest way with the least changes.

It is nice and quiet in the depot after that nasty train. I'm in such a hurry to see Rose I can hardly wait, but I guess it will be Friday before I get there if I have to lay up tonight, darn it. I do hope everything is all right at home. Tell Mr. Nall I said he must keep you and Inky cheered up.

Love to you and Inky,
Bessie

On train somewhere in Nevada
Thursday, August 26, 1915

Manly Dear,

Well I'm safely on the last lap of the journey. Was so very lucky as to get a lower tourist berth at Salt Lake and did not have to change at Ogden. Our car was just attached to the San Francisco train, but the ugly D.&R.G. [Denver & Rio

Grande] being so late hooked us on to a slow train and we are three hours late. Just sent a telegram to Rose when to meet me.

I crossed Great Salt Lake in the moonlight last night and it was the most beautiful sight I've seen yet. Miles and miles of it on each side of the train, the track so narrow that it could not be seen from the window. It looked as though the train was running on the water. I undressed and lay in my berth and watched it, the moonlight making a path of silver across the water and the farther shore so dim and indistinct and melting away into the desert as though there was no end to the lake. I thought I would watch until we came to the end of the lake, but I was so tired my eyes shut and when I opened them again it was morning and we were away out on the Nevada deserts.

I saw the sun rise on the desert as I lay in my berth and it was lovely. The bare, perfectly bare, rocky mountains in all kinds of heaps and piles as though the winds had drifted them into heaps and they had turned to rock, were purple in the hollows and rose and gold and pink on the higher places. There were yellows and browns and grays and the whole softly blended together. At the feet of the mountains lay the flat gray plain covered with sage brush, with patches of sand and alkali showing. Such a desolate dreary country even though beautiful in its way. All morning we have been going through the desert and now we are where there are piles of loose sand. All the way wherever there is a little spot of green someone is living, or perhaps I should say wherever someone is living there is a spot of green, but not always. I saw two houses and a windmill and one green bush between them. There was a river bottom for a little ways and corrals and cattle and a cowboy in red chaps driving a bunch of horses. We thought we were seeing water off at one side and I asked the porter what water it was. He laughed and said it looked like alkali beds. Then we saw them later close by, miles of perfectly white ground. In places it looked like water and then it looked like snow. There was a little house and corral right out in the middle of one big bed. Not a living creature or a green thing in sight. There was a road out and it looked like a road made in about three inches of snow with dry dirt underneath. Oh, this awful, awful country we have come to now.

This is the desert proper we have read of where people get lost in sand storms and perish of thirst. There are scattered clumps of what I think is sage brush and they are nearly buried in drifts and mounds of sand. The ground between is perfectly bare and covered with loose sand and alkali. The car and my eyes and nose are full of sand and alkali dust and everything and everyone is so dirty. We are all making a joke of it. There is a nice crowd in our car and we all talk to each other and have a good time getting acquainted. One woman talking to me this morning said they live in Kansas City and they are thinking of getting a farm. Want to trade city property. She was very much interested to know all about the Ozarks and says they will come down and see them.

We will get to San Francisco about eleven tonight. I think I have brought you up to date so will quit.

Love,
Bessie

San Francisco

San Francisco
Sunday, August 29, 1915

Manly Dear,

As you of course know* I arrived safely in San Francisco. As I walked down the walk from the train toward the ferry, Rose stepped out from the crowd and seized me.

On the ferry we sat out on the upper deck and well in front, but a fog covered the water so I did not see much of the bay except the lights around it. I was so tired anyway and I could not realize I was really here. Gillette met us as we stepped off the

---

*Laura doubtless telegraphed Almanzo.

ferry and we took a streetcar nearly home and climbed a hill the rest of the way. I went to bed soon and have been resting most of the time since.

It took all the first day to get the motion of the cars out of my head. Yesterday afternoon I went with Rose and Gillette down to the beach. We walked down the hill—all paved streets and walks and lovely buildings—to the car line and took a car to Land's End, from six to ten miles all the way through the city except for a few blocks at the last.

At Land's End I had my first view of the Pacific Ocean. To say it is beautiful does not half express it. It is simply beyond words. The water is such a deep wonderful blue and the sound of the waves breaking on the beach and their whisper as they flow back is something to dream about. I saw a lumber schooner coming in and another going out as they passed each other in the Golden Gate. They sail between here and Seattle, Washington. We walked from Land's End around the point of land and came to the Cliff House and Seal Rocks but the seals would not show themselves.

We took a side path into the parks of the Sutro Estate, which has been turned over to the city as a public park under certain conditions as to its use. The lodge near the gates and the old mansion itself were built with materials brought around the Horn in sailing ships about a hundred years ago. We went through the massive arched gateway made of stone with a life-sized lion crouched at each side and through a beautiful park of about forty acres. I don't mean we walked over it all, but we walked miles of it. The soil in these grounds was all brought to them, for originally the surface was just sand. The forest trees were all planted by this first Sutro. At every turn in the paths we came upon statues of stone, figures of men and women and animals, and birds, half hidden among the foliage of flowering plants, or peeping out from among the trees.

The house itself is built at the top of the hill. The whole front and side of the house is glass so that one would have the view from every point. The pillars of the balcony have [Delft] porcelains inset, as do the posts of the stone fence around the house. They are small squares as smooth and glossy as my china, with quaint old-fashioned pictures of children and animals, instead of the flowers on my dishes. Just think, they have stood there for a hundred years exposed to the sun and wind and weather without a stain or a crackle. Close beside the house is a very tall slender building, an observatory with a glass room at the top where the family used to go to watch the ships come in through the Golden Gate. The building is so old that it is considered unsafe and no one is allowed to go in it now.

We went from there out on the edge of the cliff where there are seats and statues around the edge and one can sit or stand and look over the ramparts across the blue Pacific. An American eagle in stone stands screaming on the edge at one side. Two cannon were in place pointing out to sea and there were several piles of cannon balls. I kicked one to be sure it was real—and it was. The winds off the ocean are delightful.

We went down on the beach where the waves were breaking. There were crowds of people there and some of them were wading. I wanted to wade. Rose said she never had but she would, so we took off our shoes and stockings and left them on the warm sand with Gillette to guard them and went out to meet the waves. A little one rolled in and covered our feet, the next one came and reached our ankles, and just as I was saying how delightful, the big one came and went above our knees. I just had time to snatch my skirts up and save them and the wave went back with a pull. We went nearer the shore and dug holes in the sand with our toes. Went out to meet the waves and ran back before the big one caught us and had such a good time.

The salt water tingled my feet and made them feel so good all the rest of the day, and just to think, the same water that bathes the shores of China and Japan came clear across the ocean and bathed my feet. In other words, I have washed my feet in the Pacific Ocean.

The ocean is not ugly. It is beautiful and wonderful.

We went from the beach to the Coast Guard or life-saving station and saw the lifeboat. Then we went to see the *Gjöa*, the only boat that has ever gone around the continent through the Northwest Passage. It is battered and worn but strong-looking still. The ship was made in Norway in 1878 and with a crew of six men and the captain was three years and four months making the journey from Norway through the Northwest Passage

GABRIEL MOULIN, SAN FRANCISCO

Ocean Beach in 1915. Land's End and the Cliff House. are in the background. This was where Laura first viewed the Pacific Ocean and first waded in salt water.

to San Francisco. The government of Norway and the Norwegians of California gave the ship to this city and left it here.*

By this time I was tired, very tired, so we took a car back to the city and stopped for dinner at a restaurant. The waiter was an Alsatian, which is a cross between a Frenchman and a German. The dinner was delicious. French bread and salmon steak and tenderloin of sole, delicious fish. I could hardly tell which was the best. Then there was some kind of an Italian dish which I liked very much, and a French strawberry pie or "tarte" which was fresh berries in a pastry shell with some kind of rich syrup poured over. There was music in the restaurant and I heard "It's a Long, Long Way to Tipperary" for the first time.

Believe me, I was tired after seeing all this in

---

*Roald Amundsen had bought this antique and modified it for use in Arctic exploratory work. He spent several winters in northern Canada frozen in, conducting scientific investigations. In the spring of 1905 he emerged from his winter quarters into open water, contacted a passing ship from San Francisco, and realized that—unintentionally—he was the first to navigate the fabled Northwest Passage. The *Gjöa* was at the Golden Gate Park until 1972, when it was returned to Norway.

one afternoon and we have been loafing all today. We went out on the walk before the house and saw Niles [an exhibition aviator] fly this afternoon. The Tower of Jewels is in sight from there too. Niles flew up and up, then dropped like an autumn leaf, floating and drifting and falling. He turned over, end over end, he turned over sideways both ways, then righted himself and sailed gracefully down.

Christopherson was flying at the beach yesterday and Rose says I shall have a flight before I go home. Gee, if it can beat wading in the ocean it will be some beat, believe me.

You know I have never cared for cities but San Francisco is simply the most beautiful thing. Set on the hills as it is with glimpses of the bay here and there and at night with the lights shining up and down the hills and the lights of ships on the water, it is like fairyland. I have not seen any of the Exposition yet. San Francisco itself would be wonderful enough for a year, but we will begin this week to go to the Fair. You must not expect me to see it all for it has been figured out that it would cost $500 just to see the five-cent, ten-cent and twenty-five-cent attractions.

BOTH: J. NIELSON ROGERS

The Vallejo Street side of the house that Rose and Gillette lived in looked much the same in this 1973 picture as it did in 1915.

The rear of the house on Vallejo Street. Carol Ann Rogers leans out of the apartment window Laura gazed through so often in September and October 1915.

Rose and Gillette have a dandy little place to live with a fine view from the windows.* It is up at the very top of a hill, with the bay in sight.

Just here Rose called to come quick and go see the fireworks at the Fair. We put on our heavy

*I visited the house in 1973. It was designed and built in the 1890's by the young architect Willis Polk, for his own use. He later became the Chairman of the Board of Architects of the 1915 Exposition. The house is at the very crown of Russian Hill and commanded a spectacular view. R.L.M.

coats and went out to the walk before the house and just a little way along it and sat down on a stone curb. The white Tower of Jewels is in sight from there. The jewels strung around it glitter and shine in beautiful colors. The jewels are from Austria and cost ninety cents each and they decorate all the cornices on the high, fancifully built tower. A searchlight is directed on the tower at night to show it off and it is wonderful.

As we looked, the aeroscope rose above the tops of the buildings. It is a chamber that can hold five hundred people. Its outlines are marked by electric lights. It is on the top of a more slender part and is lowered for the people to fill the chamber, then is raised high so they can look down on the whole Exposition at once. They have that instead of the Ferris Wheel. As it rises, it looks like some giant with a square head, craning his long neck up and up. I don't suppose it looks like that to anyone else, but that is the way it makes me feel.

Well, we sat and watched and soon a long finger of white light swept across the sky, then another and another of different colors, and then there was flashing and fading across the whole sky in that direction, the most beautiful northern-lights effect you could imagine. I think you have seen

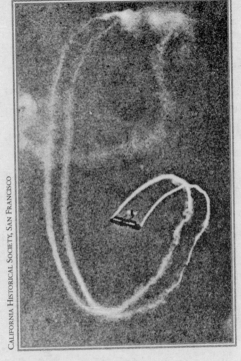

. . . . *to Loop the Loop, twice!*
Art Smith said: "I flew another 500 feet
higher, pushed the machine over into a
vertical dip, and dropped clean. When
I judged the momentum was great
enough I rammed the wheel over with
all my might. The machine turned
completely over, in a beautiful curve.
The engine picked up. I had looped my
first loop."

—*From Art Smith's autobiography*
written with Rose Wilder Lane

After Lincoln Beachey's death in March, young Art Smith, 21, was engaged as the premier exhibition flyer for the Exposition. Here he prepares to take off.

them. Well, this was more brilliant, more colors and *very* much higher on the sky. All the colors of the rainbow and some shades that I never saw the rainbow have. I have used the word "beautiful" until it has no meaning, but what other word can I use? There are forty searchlights producing this effect. Forty men handle them, producing the

*The Tower of Jewels and Exposition grounds at night.
"The illumination is gradual. First, the lower bank of
floodlights under the palms and shrubbery, next the*

*powerful tungstens in their hooded pillars, finally the
great standards flash their millions of candle power
full on the ivory façades."*

flashes in a sort of drill, under direction and orders as a drill march is done. It costs $40 a minute to show these northern lights, in salary alone. What the lights themselves cost is not for common mortals to know.

After a little of this, rockets went shooting up the beams of light, burst and fell in showers of colored stars and strings of jewels. The different colors of the searchlights were played upon the [artificially generated] steam making most beautiful and fantastic cloud shapes of different colors after the shower of stars had fallen. I do not know how long it lasted, but at last the flashes stopped and there was left the wonderful Tower of Jewels shining and glowing in the light thrown on it, and the aeroscope craning its long neck for a look down on the grounds.

I will meet some of Rose's friends this week and begin to get a line on things. Rose gets $30 a week now and she says she is saving ten percent of it, absolutely salting it down. She says it is not much but it is making a start. Gillette has worked on extra jobs for the *Call** since he came to the city, which leaves him at times without work but he has

---

*The newspaper rival of Rose's paper, the *Bulletin*.

One of the Exposition's most lovely attractions—the color illumination show and fireworks display. Amidst a shower of stars, several of the 40 searchlights produce colorful patterns on steam.

a promise of a good job as soon as a vacancy occurs, which is expected soon. Rose says they have $4,000 due them from their real estate work and that Gillette has made an assignment to us of what he owes us, but they do not know when they, or we, will get this money as the men who bought the land are unable to pay it now. The real estate business went all to smash and Stine & Kendrick* are resting till things turn.

I am so glad Mr. Nall came so soon and to get your letter. I do hope you and Inky are getting along comfortably. Take care of yourself and him, and I will look for us both as much as possible.

What a time you must have had with those chickens and that milk. I'm glad the pie was good and the thing to do was to put it in the oven. I hope you did not burn it.

Rose says tell you those fireworks are the best the world has ever known. It costs hundreds of thousands to produce them and they had experts from all over the world at work on them. She says there never was anything like them in the world except those Roman candles you got for

*The real estate agency for which Rose and Gillette had worked until a year or two before, selling land in the Sacramento Valley.

her the last Fourth of July we were in De Smet. They surpassed them, she says.*

Well, goodbye for this time. I'll go see some more to write you.

Lovingly,
Bessie

———◆———

San Francisco
September 4, 1915

Manly Dear,

So glad to get your letter and know that you were all right. My, how wet it must be back there. I'm glad we live on the hills. Mrs. Rogers is a dear, and so are you for telling me not to worry and to have a good time. But the more I see of city life the more I love the country, and listening to Gillette talk of the farming the more sure I am that the law of averages holds .here as elsewhere. Such enormous profits can be made on the farms here. Very good, he proves it, but still the farmers are unable to make the payments on their land which shows there is a leak here as everywhere.

*The Fourth of July Rose remembered must have been that of 1894. According to *On the Way Home*, the Wilder family left De Smet for a new start in Missouri later that month.

Yesterday I loafed all day. A little excitement carries me over and the next day I pay. The day before yesterday Gillette and I went to the Fair grounds in the afternoon while Rose wrote on her story. Then Rose came down in time for the illumination and fireworks and we stayed until twelve o'clock. One simply gets satiated with beauty. There is so much beauty that it is overwhelming.

The coloring is so soft and wonderful. Blues and reds and greens and yellows and browns and grays are all blended into one perfect whole without a jar anywhere. It is fairyland. We went through a large entrance gate and were in the Zone, which is a long street of attractions like the side shows at a circus, only of course not to be compared with them as they are simply wonderful. We took a seat on one of the little trains drawn by a motor and rode the length of the zone, for it is so far and there is so much walking to do. I am going again to look particularly and then I can tell you about things as I should, but on this first visit Rose and Gillette wanted me to see the Exposition as a whole and get a sort of wholesale impression.

The buildings are built like those of a city and the streets and the four corners of streets form the courts. One goes through beautiful archways in the buildings into the courts where fountains splash and lovely flowers and green things are growing. There are life-like statues and figures of animals and birds. The foundation color of the buildings is a soft gray and as it rises it is changed to the soft yellows picked out in places by blue and red and green and the eye is carried up and up by the architecture, spires and things, to the beautiful blue sky above. I have never imagined anything so beautiful.

We did not go through the buildings, leaving that for a later time, but we went into the "Forbidden Garden." There was, in the old days near a monastery, a garden where women were forbidden to go on pain of death. This is an exact copy of that old garden. The paths leading to it are dim as twilight from the shrubbery growing close over them and they are a sort of labyrinth, so that one comes suddenly and unexpectedly upon the little garden with its splashing fountain and its green grass and flowers.

I saw the Southern Pacific Railroad exhibit in their building which is a life-like reproduction of California scenes, even to the waterfalls and the blossoming orchards in the Santa Clara Valley.

The Palace of Fine Arts, by Bernard Maybeck, is the only part of the Panama Pacific international Exposition [P.P.I.E.] to survive to the present day.

"The Pioneer Mother" by Charles Grafly was the first monument to be erected in honor of the women who braved the Overland Trails.

There is one building and courts that the city is planning to keep for a museum and park.* This is where the most wonderful statuary is grouped along the walk and against the walls. "The Pioneer Mother" is one—a life-size group on a pedestal so one looks up to it. A woman in a sunbonnet, of course pushed back to show her face, with her sleeves pushed up, guiding a boy and girl before her and sheltering and protecting them with her arms and pointing the way westward. It is wonderful and so true in detail. The shoe exposed is large and heavy and I'd swear it had been half-soled.

We went to the gate to meet Rose just at dusk and then we watched the dream city light up. No lights anywhere to be seen but it was just illuminated—what is called *indirect* lighting. Then we wandered down the Zone. At the door of every show people were "ballyhooing"—doing little stunts to attract the crowd.

The Panama Canal† is wonderful on the outside. It shows the canal with a warship on guard, and the wireless station which is actually sparking and

*The Palace of Fine Arts, by the California architect Bernard Maybeck.
†This was the featured exhibit of the exposition.

sending out messages. The water flows into and out of the locks and the scenery is correct in detail, tropic of course, and the sky is someway managed by electricity so that it is twilight and the stars come out. Then they gradually pale and the sky lightens for daybreak and becomes lighter until it is daylight. They say inside there is a huge relief map and a man to explain it.

We went into the Navajo Indian village, regular cliff dwellings. It is built to be a rocky cliff and one climbs up by steps cut in the solid rock all along the way. After you get up the cliff, there are holes dug into the rock, smaller, or larger where the Indians live, making baskets and pottery and weaving rugs. They all smell like wild beast dens and I did not like to be there. The Indians are very friendly and good-natured.

We went from there to see the fireworks which I have described to you before. Seen at close range they are even more beautiful.

We peeped between the elbows of the crowd and got a glimpse of the Japanese wrestling match. Then we saw the Lantern Parade by the Japanese, which was simply a mob of Japanese carrying lanterns. Little and big men, women, and children marched by carrying Japanese lanterns. Rose made a quick move and I lost her in the crowd. I looked where Gillette had been and he was not there. I started to go in the direction I had last seen Rose and then I stood stock still. I'll admit I was terrified for the crowd was a mob and I did not know my way out. Then a hand fell on my arm and Gillette said, "All right, Mama Bess. They crowded in but I have not lost sight of you a minute. There's Rose right over there."

We went on back to the Zone and went to the Samoan village. Samoa, you know, are South Sea islands belonging to the U.S. There were several girls and men dressed, or rather undressed, in their native costume. The girls had bright silk scarves around their bodies covering their busts and waists—but leaving their shoulders bare, then short narrow skirts reaching to their knees. They wore necklaces and strings of beads and rings. The men wore the short skirts but not the cloth around the waist. Their skin was a beautiful golden color where it was not tattooed and their voices were soft and musical. The girls are very pretty and some of the men are fine-looking. They danced their native dances and sang their island songs. The girls danced by themselves, the girls and men danced together, and the men alone danced the

175

A view of the Fair from the top of the aeroscope.
The Zone is in the foreground. Seven blocks long, it
offered rides such as The Scenic Railway, A Trip to the
South Pole, A Submarine Journey; attractions such as
the Chinese Pagoda (center); a small Celestial City
housing a restaurant, theater, and shop; and shows
such as Madame Ellis, mind reader, and Captain, the
educated horse.

176

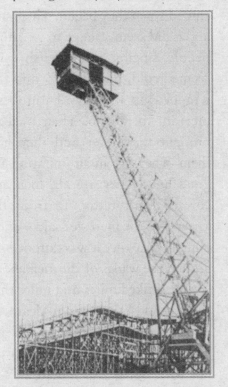

The aeroscope, capable of lifting passengers 285 feet from its base.

dance of the headhunters with long ugly knives. In all this dancing and singing they never touched each other and they danced in every muscle of their bodies, even their fingers and toes. They were very graceful and I did enjoy every bit of it. At the very last they all sang "It's a Long, Long Way to Tipperary." They all seemed very much pleased with themselves that they could sing it and all smiled when they began. Their singing is beautiful and it did seem strange to see those strange, island people singing the English battle song. They seemed cold, poor things, and they left the stage wrapped up in heavy bathrobes. They are very pleasant to talk to. Their own real live princess brought them over and they have a chief with them. They live in an imitation Samoan village of grass huts. They are all, men and women alike, covered with tattooing from the waist to the knees—so the manager said—and when I caught a glimpse of a knee it was tattooed and it also showed around the waists of the men above the skirt.

We walked miles and miles that afternoon and evening and I was tired to death.

I am disgusted with this letter. I have not done halfway justice to anything I have described. I can not with words give you an idea of the wonderful beauty, the scope and grandeur of the Exposition. But I will see it more in detail soon and tell you more about it.

I hope everything is going along all right, and that Inky still keeps his appetite. How are the chickens and the pigs and everything? Truly, I am enjoying myself but I am also missing Rocky Ridge. Believe me, I am glad we have such a beautiful home.

I am being lazy and resting but Rose says it is not expected that one will recover from the trip in less than a week. I do not know why I had to make so many changes. The trains I was on simply did not go any farther and I had to change. Rose says she thinks it must have been because of the increase in passenger traffic.

Love,
Bessie

—⁓—

San Francisco
September 7, 1915

Manly Dear,

I have taken tea in a Chinese tea room in Chinatown and went through some of their shops looking at the curious things they have for sale. It

Chinatown in 1915.

is very interesting to walk through Chinatown as we do when we walk down town from Rose's place. There are such wonderful hand carvings of ivory and stone and wood in the windows, beautiful hand embroideries and tapestry. Then there are the fish markets with such large fish and small fish, with lobsters and octopus and stingaree and live turtles and shrimps and funny and lovely fish that we do not know the names of. The streets are full of the Chinese people of course. A good many of them are wearing American dress and are very nice looking people. Some still wear the Chinese costume as it is in pictures you have seen and the children are the cutest ever. I do not like the Chinese food and shall not try any more of it.

We went for dinner to an Italian restaurant in Little Italy, the part of town where the Italians live. It was a funny little restaurant where we could sit and watch the cooking done and the proprietor himself cooked or waited or did whatever was necessary. His wife waited on the tables and there were other waiters and help with the cooking. The room was full of people eating and not a word of English was spoken except by Rose and myself, except when the proprietor struggled to take our order. Everyone was talking and a group of men got excited and talked loudly at each other. I'm sure they were talking about the war. The food was fine, though I could not tell you the name of it, and it was all very interesting indeed.

I am sure by now you are trying to find the ear spoon, and cannot, so I am sending you a Chinese ear spoon,* toothpick, and a fork to eat with. I am so sorry about Inky missing me so much and I am afraid it will only make him feel worse if I send him a letter! I am enjoying my visit and the sightseeing so much but still it seems as though I have been away from Rocky Ridge for a year. Do take care of yourself and everything. We are going out to the Exposition to spend the day tomorrow. I am tired today and resting.

What an awful time you must be having with so much rain. Oh, did you see in the papers about Pettirossi† falling into the bay with his flying machine? He was not hurt.

Lovingly,
Bessie

---

*To clean out the ears. The Chinese stores in San Francisco stocked them in silver, gold, and jade.
†Silvio Pettirossi was a flier from the Argentine who completed a brief engagement at the Fair. The airport in Asunción, Paraguay, is named after him.

I'll bring you the ear spoon after all. I'm afraid it would get broken in the letter.

———— ∿ ————

San Francisco
September 8, 1915

Manly Dear,

I must tell you of the delightful day I spent yesterday. Rose and I went down town in the morning and Rose turned in her copy at the *Bulletin* office. We had a few errands to do and then we had a cup of tea and some muffins at "The Pig 'n' Whistle"—a tea room. Gillette does not come home at noon so we did not, but took the tea and muffins for our lunch. After that we walked out to the top of "Telegraph Hill."

To reach it one goes through the Italian tenement district where the Italian fishermen live, and goes up a steep hill, so steep that there are cleats across the walk in places to help in the climb. From the top of Telegraph Hill we looked down on the bay and boats and ships of all kinds going in every direction. Away out in the bay we saw what looked like a house bobbing over the water and we watched it until it came close enough so we could see that it was a houseboat being towed by a little tug. Across the bay we could see some of the cities of Oakland and Berkeley. In other directions we could see nothing but water. When we tired of this we went down the hill on the other side to the waterfront, among the docks. Most of the docks are covered and look like long warehouses running out in the bay with ships tied up on each side of them. After awhile we came to an open dock, piled full of lumber. We walked out to the end and watched the waves and looked at the military prison of Alcatraz on the island. There were fourteen sailing ships anchored in sight and three big ferry ships. One coast steamer went out for its voyage up or down the coast and several motor boats went by. This is a wonderful harbor, so large and quiet, with room for so many ships to anchor safely, and such a narrow, well-protected entrance: the Golden Gate.

I watched the water until I felt as though the pier were rocking, then we came back and went on down the shore. We passed two launches from the battleships and the sailors from one had turned their pet black goat out on the wharf for a run. We gave him plenty of room. I was afraid he would not know how to treat women. A little farther on we came to some Italian fishermen mending their nets and when we asked they told us where the fishermen's wharf was and we went on down to it. There were so many fishing boats tied up. Some of them were unloading fish and, oh, I wish you could see the fish. There were great piles of them and they were being weighed and carted away and taken into the fish markets nearby. Some were great salmon that would weigh from thirty to sixty pounds. We could buy one weighing about twenty-five pounds for sixty cents. They told us that they went out to the fishing about three o'clock in the morning and we are going down some morning and see them start. Everyone was so pleasant and gentlemanly. When we could tear ourselves away we went on to the California Fruit Association's cannery.

Before I forget it, though, I must tell you that Gillette saw a fifty-pound salmon the other morning that a man had caught with a hook and line. Some fishing?

Well, we went all through the cannery and my doubts about the cleanness of canned goods from a large plant are removed. I felt hungry for the canned fruit right there. It was *clean*. I will tell you about it when I come. It is so long to write. We went all over it. Everyone working there was Italian and I guess there were a couple of hundred girls and don't know how many men. They were so kind and nice to us and when they could not speak English they would chatter Italian at us and smile. After going through the cannery we walked to a streetcar line and came home. Rose figures we had walked ten miles altogether.

Pitch my letters into the bathroom and when I come I'll look them over and tell you more about these things.

Lovingly,
Bessie

—⁓—

San Francisco
September 11, 1915

Dear Manly,

This is just another chapter of my last letter. I forgot to tell you that the highest fort in the world is on one post of the Golden Gate. You see, the ocean comes up on the outside, and between two high mountains is a comparatively narrow passage into the harbor of the bay. This narrow passage is the Golden Gate and the fort is on the mainland side. There is no sign of the fort to be seen. The defenses are disappearing guns, and the fort is the highest in the world. The harbor is perfectly protected for that is the only way in.

From my bedroom window today I counted fifteen ships in sight at one time on the bay. One of them is a battleship and there are three cruisers. There are two other battleships out by the Golden Gate. One of them is the *Maine*.* They are in battle paint, grim and gray. The cruisers are white. When we were out at the beach we saw the fastest mail and passenger ship on the Pacific, outward bound. From the gate in front of where Rose lives one can see nine towns, the smallest larger than Springfield and some of them larger than Kansas City. They are scattered along the stretch of bay which can be seen. There is also a great number of ships always in sight, and three islands—Goat Island, Angel Island, Alcatraz Island. The military prison is on Alcatraz Island.

By the way, if you and Mr. Nall care to read Rose's story, "Ed Monroe, Man Hunter," you may do so knowing that all the stories in it, although incidents, are true, and *actually happened*. "Ed Monroe" came to dinner with us and told Rose those stories for her to use until after midnight. Instead of being an old detective, he is an old crook who has served time more than once.

*Not the original *Maine* sunk in Havana in 1898.

He was a burglar who did the high-class work, jewelry robberies, etc. He is straight now and working in the circulation department [of the *Bulletin*]. He is very interesting and of course his name is not the one used in the story. He strung Rose's pearls for her, the ones I brought her, you know. He said it was his old trade, the restringing and resetting of jewels—when he had stolen them, I suppose.

Rose was much pleased over the little bottle of possum oil and is going to keep it for a curiosity. She has been about sick ever since I came with a bad cold, but I've been dosing her with snake root* and think she will be all right now.

I went down to the *Bulletin* twice with her this morning. We walked down through Little Italy and Chinatown and the Japanese section. It was very interesting and the shops were so full of strange things in the windows. We just walked through so I could see some of the people and get a general idea of it. The old Chinatown is gone, you know,† and the buildings look on the outside like any

---

*There are many varieties of snake root growing in the U.S., and all have been put to one medicinal use or another. Evidently Laura brought her own and steeped it into a tea for Rose.

†It was destroyed in the great earthquake and fire of 1906.

other. Soon we are going down and rummage in the shops and eat in some of the restaurants, and then I can write you more about it.

Please save my letters. I might want to use some of the descriptions later and I also wish you would ask Mrs. Weed for Mrs. Comstock's address. I was going to bring it with me and forgot.

Gillette has planned to take me into the valley where they raise so much poultry—white leghorns. It has become current report that the poultry men are not making their expenses, but one man there whom Gillette knows has ten thousand hens on fifteen acres. Three men take care of them and he says he makes $1.38 a year on each hen.

He says the reason the others are not making expenses is because they do not work hard enough, that it takes *Work* to care for hens properly and that they drive in their automobiles too much when they should be working. I want to see how he handles so many hens and I think I'll get a chance to go.

Have you turned the hogs into the orchard yet and did they like it? Will they leave the green feed and come up for their dose of medicine?

Love,

Bessie

San Francisco
September 13, 1915

Manly Dear,

I am perched on the side of Telegraph Hill watching the ships go by. There are twenty-six ships in sight and ten small sail boats. One of them is a hay boat. It looks like a load of hay floating on the water with three sails on it. There are about three thousand tons of hay on board, one thousand down below decks and the two thousand on deck. It looks strange to see a load of hay floating on the water. It has come down some river from the alfalfa farms. Just now a British trading ship is going past outward bound, perhaps to be sunk by a German submarine. It is the freight steamers, you know, that they particularly want to get. It has gone past now and I hear the blast of its whistle. I suppose it is meeting some other ship. Now in the immediate foreground is a white ferry steamer and farther over an orange-colored Exposition ferry bound for the Exposition grounds. There are two lumber ships going by loaded with lumber. One of them is coming in to the pier. It is loaded a little unevenly and tips some to one side. I suppose it

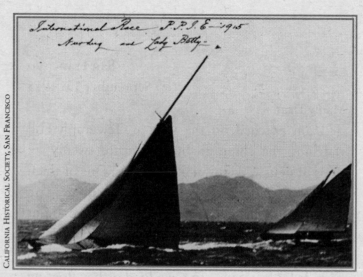

One of the yacht races held during the Exposition in San Francisco Bay.

Ferryboats in San Francisco Bay at the time of Laura's visit. One similar to these, on which Laura may have been a passenger, can be visited on the shorefront in San Diego.

The wharves as Laura saw them, with Alcatraz in the background.

lists to starboard or to larboard or something. One sailing ship with dirty-looking sails with clean new patches on them has sailed in and dropped anchor. The sails are running down. Now someone is getting over the side into a little boat. This ship looks like a tramp and I think it is. A ship is going by now that came from the Hawaiian Islands with a cargo of sugar. It is empty and riding high in the water. A Hawaiian passenger ship has passed bound for the Hawaiian Islands and Uncle Sam's gray battleship is lying anchored a little way out. Little white yachts are scurrying among the larger ships. There are six piers in sight with all kinds of ships tied up to them. One is a British freighter with the flag flying, glad to be safe for awhile I suppose. Another is a Greek ship with several strings of flags flying in the wind. They say that is a sign that it will leave soon.

The hills across the bay look beautiful through the fog and Berkeley and Oakland show dimly. The tide is rising now and pouring in through the Golden Gate. I can see just how far it has come in by the white caps on the water. Goat Island is right in front. That is where the naval training school is.

One little sailing boat has just gone by, sailing

so close into the wind* that the tip of the sail touches the water now and then. The man in sight is standing on the other edge of the boat, out on the very edge to keep it from tipping over. But I could watch these ships go by and write you about them all day. Rose is thinking of moving out here. There is a little house she can rent which faces all this. It is built on the side of the hill and there is a balcony overhanging the steep hillside. It looks over the roofs of the houses below, and the piers and all the beautiful bay is spread out like a picture. An artist friend of Rose's, a dear girl, is moving into another little house right next to the one Rose can get. The places are rather dilapidated but can be fixed very cozily.

I am glad Inky is more cheerful and that you are getting along all right. Rose and I are going to do some work on stories together this week.

Lovingly,
Bessie

I forgot to say that there is a wireless station on Goat Island. I can see the mast. From there they talk to Honolulu in the Hawaiian Islands. I saw a yacht race this afternoon too. Twenty-one little sail

*Laura must have meant "so close-hauled."

boats with their white sails filling out with the wind came into sight like a flock of white ducks. They sailed to a certain point, then turned and raced back out of sight behind the headland. It was very pretty.

Rolf Pelkie who has drawn pictures for the *Bulletin* has disappeared without a word of warning. The rumor among the newspaper people is that he was a German spy.*

———————

San Francisco
September 13, 1915

Manly Dear,

About the horse—if it is the horse you want I suppose it would be a good plan to change a horse as old as Buck for a six-year-old. The $50 you would give to boot, you would just be giving for the colt and it would soon be the third horse for the farm, or would sell and buy the third horse. However, be sure the mare is the horse you want so you will not be out of a team.

*He wasn't. His absence is unexplained, but he returned to the city for a long and successful career. Rumors of spying and sabotage by the Kaiser's agents were on the rise in 1915, and some of them were borne out later.

What a shame to have the grapes stolen. Have you any idea who it was?

Honest fact, I'm homesick but there are so many interesting things still to be seen and I am here, that I feel I must see some more of them before I leave. Then I do want to do a little writing with Rose to get the hang of it a little better so I can write something that perhaps I can sell.

Don't buy the horse unless you are sure it is gentle. I do not want you hurt while I am gone or any other time for that matter. Could you get it on trial? What about getting a horse at a sale? If there has been so much washing away of crops, etc., perhaps there will be a good many sales—$125 is not a bargain, but full price unless the price of horses has advanced. But you are on the ground. Do whatever you think best.

I am going to do the things I absolutely must do before I come home. There are a few, you know, such as going over some of my copy with Rose and going out to the Fair a couple more times, and then I am coming home. Rose is very busy with her copy and the house and all, so we do not accomplish much in a day. I am doing what she will let me to help so she will have time to help me and to go play at the Fair with me. I am anxious to get back and take charge of the hens again. Believe me, there is no place like the country to live and I have not heard of anything so far that would lead me to give up Rocky Ridge for any other place.

I want to go to Petaluma and see the chicken farm but that will cost something and I may not do that.

Anyhow, I'm sure that together we can figure out easier ways of doing the chicken work when you have a little time to fix things. I hope nothing happens there to make my trip overly expensive for it has done me lots of good and I think it has done Rose good too. Gee! It will be good to get busy again on my job.

Love to Inky & yourself,
Bessie

—————

San Francisco
September 15, 1915

Manly Dear,

I am sending you [Rose's] printed story of something that Rose and I actually saw and heard on the Zone.

Yesterday Gillette and I went to the Presidio,

the army reservation where the soldiers live in barracks and in tents. There are beautiful residences where the officers live and a wide cement drive where automobiles and carriages go, with dirt roads for the cavalry. We arrived by the guardhouse just in time to see them bring out the prisoners.

All this soldier place is along the shore out where the disappearing guns guard the Golden Gate. They looked ugly, crouched in their hiding place behind the hills. We could see them but were not allowed to go close to them. Big signs said "Unauthorized persons will be detained by the sentinels." We saw at least fifty of these huge iron monsters, twelve- and sixteen-inch guns, and there were batteries hidden behind woods and one great encampment with batteries where we could not even go inside the wire enclosure to see any signs of the guns. There were smaller guns on wheels scattered around and an enormous searchlight on wheels. It was under cover but the great doors were open and men were working to make it even more spick and span than it already was. It was close beside the cement road which runs all the way around the edge of the cliffs, at the foot of which is the ocean.

Just across the narrow part where the passage

is from the ocean to the gulf, were four forts on the other side, one of which is the highest fort in the world. We saw the stables where the cavalry horses and the mules are kept. Any number of horses and mules are tied on each side of a long rope stretched across the yards and immense barns. They all looked fat and well cared for. We met soldiers on foot, on horseback, and saw them at work at different things. Everyone seemed to be busy about their affairs and everything was so clean and well kept.

Gillette has a friend who is a lieutenant in the Navy and he has given Gillette his card with a note on the back saying to show him every courtesy. This will throw the battleship wide open to us, as he is next to the highest in rank on the ship. They will take special pains to show us and explain to us and we three are planning to go out tomorrow. This lieutenant holds the world's record for marksmanship with the big guns on a battleship and is in charge of the reserves at the naval training school on Goat Island.

I did not write you particularly of the time we spent at the Fair, for I saw so much that I could not describe it all. Rose and I are going out this afternoon. We are going to see the livestock exhibit and the "Dogs of All Nations." Then we are going on board a launch and sail out into the ocean to meet the sunset. Then we are coming back and stay on the Zone until they put us out, about eleven. The Zone is filled with a crowd of merrymakers and is full of music and lights and funny things. I am making notes in a book of the different things I see at the Exposition and when I come home I can describe them to you.

Rose has finished her story and has now to write another and have it all finished in nineteen days when they will begin to publish it.

Love,
Bessie

ENCLOSED NEWSPAPER CLIPPING

SAILORS AT SEA ON THE ZONE

They were five sailors, and they had come on shore for a good time.

You could see by their eager, determined expressions that they meant it to be a very good time indeed—a really memorable time that would color with happy recollections a long voyage at sea.

And they had hastened with eager feet to the Zone.

But the Zone is a bewildering place to be when one is looking for *a* good time—there are so many good times on every hand.

And the five sailors were obliged to choose ONE—at least, one to begin with.

Here were the barkers—"Watch him! Watch him! He's foxy! He's foxy!"

And the spielers—"This way! This way! Carnival of music and mirth!"

And the ballyhoos—"Tum! Tum! Tum! Whoopee! Al-la-ah-hooOO! See the hula-hula-hula-hula!"

The five sailors hesitated, and dodged the Irish jaunting car. They hesitated again, and were accosted by the Waffle Clown. They moved down the street and conferred together.

"The Streets of Cairo suits me," said one.

"We've bloomin' well seen the real thing. I want to see something new—say we try the Educated Horse," said another.

"'E's tame. I vote we go to the Forty-Niners."

"I 'ear they sell nawthin' but soft drinks. Let's see the 'Uman Midgets."

And so they conferred, coming to no conclusion.

Until suddenly five pairs of roving eyes

caught sight of the one irresistible attraction. For a moment they stood and gazed, and listened. Then, in single file, with beaming faces and not a dissenting murmur, they approached the ticket booth and purchased tickets, they mounted the sloping approach to the platform, passed the ticket-taker, and began a hilarious round of giddy joy.

The five sailors had finally found the one attraction on the Zone irresistible to them.

And they had paid their dimes at the "Old Red Mill" for a boat ride.

———

San Francisco
September 21, 1915

Manly Dear,

Yesterday I saw the "Dogs of All Nations" and was rather disappointed in them. There were some interesting ones, among them some of Perry's team who went to the North Pole. Then there was an Irish Wolf Hound, which breed the man in charge said was very rare. The one we saw was as large as a yearling steer and was only thirteen months old and thin. They said he was worth $3,000, perhaps like Mr. Quigley's thousand-dollar one, but this one was certainly a monster. It seemed impossible that it could be a dog and be so large.

We saw some fine Percheron horses and some Belgian horses and the dearest little Hungarian ponies. They are the size of Shetlands. One was a dapple gray with silver mane and tail. He was beautiful. The man said he was worth $500. While he was having the pony play around on the end of the halter a man came by with a very large Belgian horse and they looked so funny as they passed by each other.

There were some lovely Kentucky race and riding horses, and believe me, they can all have their automobiles that want them. I would have me a Kentucky riding horse if I could afford it.

And OH I saw the Carnation milk cows being milked with a milking machine. And it milked them clean and the cows did not object in the least. The man in charge took your address and if you get any literature be sure and save it, for this machine is certainly a success and I can tell you about it when I come.

I have had a trip on the bay out into the sunset. It was wonderful and the more the boat rolled on the waves the better I liked it. I did not get dizzy at all. We went out to the highest fort in the world and around by the quarantine station on Angel Island and then back to the anchorage. The fog rolled up and came down on us and we could not see the land in any direction. The ocean swell came in through the Golden Gate and rocked the boat and we could imagine we were away out on the ocean. It was just a little steam yacht we were on and Rose and I stood up in the very front and let the spray and the mist beat into our faces and the wind blow our hair and clothes and the boat roll under our feet and it was simply glorious.

Since then we have taken the ferry boat and gone down the bay to Sausalito. We took a loaf of bread with us and threw it to the sea gulls and they followed us clear across the bay. We would throw a piece of bread out and they would try to catch it but it usually fell into the water and then they would drop down after it and squall and try to get it away from each other. I enjoyed the boat ride very much but it was not so good as the other because the boat was larger and would not pitch. We got off at Sausalito and stayed over two boats.

We walked around the town, which is built all up and down the sides of the hills and the streets are crooked and no two houses built on the same level. It is a beautiful little place.

It was getting twilight when we took the boat back and we went out and up the path of the moon on the waves. We counted thirty-one ships and small motorboats anchored in the harbor as we came away. It was a beautiful sight, and we stood out on the deck as close as we could get to the water all the way home.

The lights at the Exposition made it look like fairyland and the lights of the city rising on the hills, row after row behind, linked it all with the stars until one could not tell where the lights stopped and the stars began. San Francisco is a beautiful, wonderful city and the people in it all seem so friendly—I mean the people one meets on the streets who are perfect strangers.

There seems to be a spirit of comradeship and informality among men and women alike. I thought it was because of the Fair but Rose says it is always that way. Perhaps it is because of the fire when they all got so well acquainted.

Sunday we went for a twelve-mile streetcar ride in all directions over the city and it only cost us a nickel apiece because of transfers.

We saw the old mission that was the first of San Francisco,* founded by the priest who put the stone cross on the hill for the ships at sea. This old mission church is decorated by the Indians of those early days. The rafters and beams of the ceiling are stained in Indian designs and the pictures and wall decorations are the work of the Indians also. Before the mission runs the "King's Road" which reached all up and down the coast.† It was traveled in those days by the priests as they went from one mission to another and of course by Indians and others. There were bells on all the highest points and there was a system of ringing the bells in such a way as to carry news from point to point so that it could travel all up and down the coast.

After we left the mission we went on out five miles to where they are starting a new suburb of the city. There is a beautiful view of the bay. Then we came back through Butcher Town and passed the China Basin and up town again where we stopped at a moving picture show and saw Charlie Chaplin,

---

*Mission Dolores, nucleus of the city, originally the Mission of Saint Francis of Assisi.

†El Camino Real, the highway built by the Spanish colonists then ruled by Carlos III.

who is horrid. I mean we saw him act in the pictures.

I am tired and must go to bed early so I can go to San Jose tomorrow. Besides I must leave something to tell you when I come home or you will not be glad to have me.

Lovingly,
Bessie

The foghorn on Alcatraz is crying out at regular intervals so it must be that the fog is getting thick. Every few minutes I hear the bellow of a steamer's whistle as it comes in or meets or passes another boat. The foghorn on Alcatraz is the most lonesome sound I ever heard and I don't see how the prisoners on the island stand it.

~~~

San Francisco
September 21, 1915

Manly Dear,

Rose is running around town getting the material together for another story and I have just come back from seeing the Germans capture Przemys*

*During World War I this city, a former Austrian fortress, fell to the Russians in 1915 but was retaken by Germany that same year.

in a moving picture theater. The pictures are true, being actually taken on the ground. It is horrible because it looks so implacable, so absolutely without mercy. I saw the big siege guns in action and saw them rock on their bases when they were fired. The Germans dropped 700,000 shells on the Russian position in four hours. They fired from the four sides. It is no wonder the men can not stand and face such shells especially as they (the guns) are always so far out of reach. These were ten miles away.

Tomorrow Rose and I are going to see the Santa Clara Valley and San Jose. This is one valley where they have the sea breeze and Rose thinks we might like to live there.* I would not think of living in an interior valley. It is a worse heat than Florida and it is all the year around. I saw and felt it as I came, you know. I asked Rose and she said she would not live herself where she could not get the sea breezes.

The first of next week we are going to Mill Valley, which is up the bay and the breezes come. Land can be had there for two to three hundred an acre. The place is really a suburb of San Francisco

---

*Apparently Rose had been trying to persuade her mother to consider moving to California with Almanzo.

and San Francisco would be our market. There are a few miles by rail and then across the bay on the ferry. Rose and Gillette both say that we could make our living on an acre raising eggs for the San Francisco market and have the most of what we could get for the [Mansfield] farm out at interest. Eggs are now forty-five cents and the farmer is getting forty-two, but I have not yet been able to find out what the poultry men have to pay for the feed. Rose says we will ask some of them when we go to the place. The big poultry raising place of California is just fifteen miles from Mill Valley. It is called Petaluma. They also say that I could write here as well or better than I can there, but that, you know, is very uncertain. Anyhow, I am going to see it and find out all I can about it and the Santa Clara Valley, then I can tell you when I come home and we can decide whether we will look into it any more.

Rose is planning to buy a lot in Mill Valley and build a little place to live and so stop rent. She says she can pay [what she now pays in] rent toward the place and have the place left, while now she pays the money out and has nothing to show for it.

Gillette has no regular job but gets extra work whenever he can, and has some good prospects for work, but just now Rose is carrying them both. She is getting $30 a week but the house rent and the bills take it nearly all. It costs every time one turns around. Even the car-fare counts up for they have to go all over town about their work and the distances are too great to walk. Rose had to give up moving to Telegraph Hill. We found out that the landlady, who lives next door with seven children, gets drunk and fights. Not a good neighborhood, you see, and that is why the rent was lower.

I got to San Francisco with $15 left. I have not spent any of it since I got here and Rose gave me $10 yesterday to give to you when I get home. She gave it to me for keeping and said she thought she could spare it. Of course if anything should go wrong to make expenses more, or there should be any change in her job before I leave, she might have to have it back, but she thinks not and says she intends to do as she said and make up to you for what you are losing by my being away.

If Gillette lands a regular job as he expects, he says he will lift the $500 [mortgage] that is on the [Mansfield] place but I think we must not count on that for of course anything is uncertain until it is landed. However, if Rose does make out to give us something for my time and things go right, perhaps we can pay a hundred on the $200 note, and then if the hens will help us worry that out this winter then the $250 which Gillette has secured to us on his commissions will half pay the note on the farm.* I am being as careful as I can and I am not for a minute losing sight of the difficulties at home or what I came for. Rose and I are blocking out a story of the Ozarks for me to finish when I get home. If I can only make it sell, it ought to help a lot and besides, I am learning so that I can write others for the magazines. If I can only get started at that, it will sell for a good deal more than farm stuff. We are slow about it, for Rose has to do the work that draws her pay. I do the housework so that she will have time to help me with my learning to write and to go with me to see the things that I must see before I go away.

I do enjoy being with Rose but I am so homesick it hurts. Rose has worked so hard to save the money to get me out for the visit that it seems a shame to leave before my ticket expires, but I am going to try and get things done so that I can come home the middle of October, which will be about three weeks yet if I have it right. I will not be able

*It seems likely that Rose and Gillette had borrowed $250 from Laura and Manly to get started.

to see Thirkield's brother. Sacramento is too long a railroad trip to take just for that. I came through there when I came here but am going back another way.

Mrs. Cobb is away off my line of travel coming home. I would like to see her very much but I do not feel that I can pay what it would cost. Places are so far apart out here—people do not realize. These mountains are like walls and on the train one climbs and climbs and then comes almost back to where he was before.

Rose wants very much to save enough so that she can go with me and start me home by way of Los Angeles. To do that I will have to lose this end of my ticket and it will cost my fare and hers down and hers back. That is if we do as we want and go by steamer. It is my only chance to have a trip on the ocean. Any other will cost too much. I am rather afraid I will have to give that up but if I do manage to go that way I will see Mrs. Comstock and West if I can find him. I know it must be hard for you and I feel guilty to have come, but I'll help you all I can when I get back and try to tell you all I have seen and you will not have to cook any more.

Mrs. Cooley must have been a sight, and if you don't mind I would rather not dress that way.

I like to get your letters but of course I do not expect you to write when you have so much to do. Just a card or a word now and then so I will know you are all right. I have not had a word from De Smet and I have written them twice. Once when I first got here, and then again telling them I had heard from you and asking how Ma was.*

Be good to Inky and yourself and take care of things the best you can. I do hope nothing will go very wrong until I get back and not then of course. I hope Mr. Nall came back. I hate to think of you alone.

Your loving Bessie

———⚬———

POSTCARD
(PICTURE OF RIDGWAY'S TEA EXHIBIT,
FOOD PRODUCTS BUILDING)

September 22, 1915

Dear Papa—Showed Bessie the dogs and cows and horses. Saw a milking machine. We are sending literature about it. Save it. This week we are

---

*Laura's father had died, but her mother was living in De Smet with Mary, Laura's sister.

going down into the Santa Clara Valley and show Bessie California orchards. Wish you were here. Tell Inky not to be jealous. We did not see any dogs we liked better than him.

Rose

San Francisco
September 23, 1915

Dear Manly,

I am very tired this morning after my trip seeing the Santa Clara Valley yesterday. I started at 8:30 in the morning, rode for half an hour on the streetcar and then one and one half hours on the train. This brought us to San Jose. Rose showed me around the city for awhile. I like the town very much. We had lunch at a restaurant and then took a jitney bus for Los Gatos. From there we went to Palo Alto by electric streetcar and there took the train back to San Francisco, getting home about seven o'clock in the evening. I enjoyed it but am glad I am not going anywhere today.

The trip took us clear around the valley so that I saw all parts of it. It is a beautiful place to look at if one likes to see very intensive orchard raising and handling. The bottom of the valley is as level as a floor and the foothills rising to mountains completely surround it except for the side open to the bay and the ocean breezes. It was very, very hot in the sun but cool in the shade and with a cool breeze blowing. Most of the valley is in orchard and the trees are of course set with mathematical precision, all trimmed to exactly the same shape and form, all the same size and the ground beneath them all as smooth and bare as a very flat smooth garden spot. The trees are trimmed in the shape of an inverted cone and are trimmed back so that they do not grow tall. They make no shade that one could stand in to rest a moment. The orchards are all irrigated of course. Ditches are plowed through the orchards in the spring and the water is run through them every six weeks through the bearing season. Then after that the ground is plowed smooth and is left that way for awhile. They are just now beginning to plow the ditches and let the water in again for the fall irrigation. It looked ugly to me, someway, to see the men working in the hot sun letting the water into the ditches so it would run around the feet of the tree while the tree itself and all its leaves were loaded with dust from the plowing. They did look as though they wanted a drink so much.

I saw some dairy farms which looked about as they might anywhere except that they too were dry and dusty. There were some chicken ranches, but the hens here are all kept in runs that are perfectly bare ground. The green stuff is cut and fed them and to me they looked dusty, hot and unhappy, though I suppose they were well cared for and comfortable.

The farm houses are fine and the places look prosperous. The roads are splendid and the little towns are lovely. The mountains which can be seen in the distance or close up, according as to where one is, are very beautiful, with the changing fog around them. However, I would not like to live there for I do not enjoy the heat and the dust, and the flat, flat land is tiresome to look at. You would like that to work, of course, but we could not get any good land for less than $500 an acre and from all I can find out I do not believe it would be the best thing to do even if one had money enough. [The threat of] prohibition is ruining the grape industry of California and it is only a question of a little time when the grape grower will go out of the business except, of course, those who furnish fresh grapes for eating.

Five hundred dollars an acre is too much to pay for land to farm on, even in California. If we had the thousand dollars I would rather put it at interest than buy two acres of land to work hard on. Wouldn't you?

I am going to see the land around Mill Valley and find out all I can about it. Then if I come home by way of Los Angeles I will see about the country there, and at Pasadena, but I truly believe that when I come home and talk it all over with you we will decide to be satisfied where we are and figure out some way to cut down our work and retire right there. Gillette is trying to make me see how we could come out here and do scientific farming on a couple of acres at a great deal more profit, but we would have it all to learn and we are rather old dogs to learn new tricks, especially as we do not have to do so. The more I see here the more I think that I will come home and put all my attention on the chickens.

I am getting some pointers on how to handle more of them for of course there will need to be more in order to get much from it, but if I can make $1 a year on a hen there, why be to all the trouble to move out here and learn new conditions when that is about all they make here? And if I would have to keep 1500 chickens or more to make a success here I do not see why I can not handle as many there, and all without the trouble of moving. We can either make you comfortable in spite of the cold in some way or let you go south to spend the coldest weather.

Oh, I hope you are fairly comfortable and can get help to take care of the crop so we will have the chicken feed for this year. It is fine that the stuff grew so well. Feed the hens some linseed meal so they will grow their feathers before cold weather. The laying ration, you know, is four parts of bran, two of corn chop, one of bone and one half of oil meal. I suppose you are giving them all the bone they want as we always do, and I believe I would increase the oil meal to get them to grow their feathers. If there are any sunflower seeds give them to the hens now. That helps with the feathers too.

Gillette and Rose will get their deferred commissions soon or find out that the men can not make their payments, in which case they will lose them. I think if I am on the ground when Gillette gets his I can get the $250 he owes us. If I am not here to strike when the iron is at the right heat I do not know whether we will get any more than the $250 or not. He will have enough if he gets it so that he can lend it to us and he says he will, but money runs through his fingers like water and he might not get around to send it to me until it was all gone.

I have the battleship yet to see and Mill Valley and then I am through with sight-seeing. Oh, of course there are things here that I would love to see, enough to last a year, but I will have seen all I am very particular about. I want to finish blocking out my story but I will likely have that done by the time the sight-seeing is over and then I will break away and come home.

Rose has a very hard assignment from the paper now and it is keeping her busy at work. She was sent on our trip yesterday and I just went along. Today she is at the office while I am resting.

Gillette has worked for the last few days covering a couple of conventions for a press syndicate. Just a short job. He has not yet managed to get on permanently anywhere. It is my private opinion that the State of California is seeing hard times even though they will not admit it. I am sure that business is dull in a good many ways, from the talks we had with the real estate man yesterday and other straws.

Lovingly,
Bessie

―――≈≈≈―――

POSTCARD

San Francisco
September 24, 1915

Dear Manly,

This is some of the country I saw on trip to San Jose, only the orchards are not in bloom now. Address my letters 1019 B. Vallejo St., San Francisco.

Bessie

―――≈≈≈―――

San Francisco
September 28, 1915

Manly Dear,

I did not get Wilhelm's letter so I suppose I missed one of yours too. I think they are rather careless with the mail at the office and so you had better send the letters to the house. Address them until further notice to 1019 B. Vallejo St., San Francisco.

Sunday afternoon I went over to Berkeley on the ferry steamer, about seven miles across the bay. We had a little lunch with us and ate it up on the top of one of the Berkeley hills. It is lovely crossing the bay. I always get at the front of the boat and on the lower deck to be as near the water as possible. Then I stand and hold to the rope and let the boat lift and sway under my feet and the spray and wind beat in my face and watch the gulls. After we cross the bay we take an electric train which is out on the end of the long pier.

I must tell you about these piers reaching out into the bay. The water is shallow on that side and they are dredging from the bottom of the bay and taking the rock and dirt to build out the shore. It is made land for one mile out now where these piers run and they are filling in between the piers. There are several of the piers. Oh, I don't know how many, a dozen I should guess. The cities of Oakland and Berkeley are doing the work and they have appropriated $10,000,000 to build land out as far as Goat Island, which is about another mile, making two miles in all of made land. They are doing this to save five minutes in time from

Oakland and Berkeley to San Francisco. Oakland is once and a half again as large as Kansas City, and Berkeley is about as large as Oakland, but they are really suburbs of San Francisco and if it were not for the bay they would be all one city. People live in Oakland and Berkeley and come every morning to their down town places of business in the city (San Francisco) and it is to save the five minutes on each trip every day for these people that the $10,000,000 is to be spent.

Berkeley is the "city of homes" and is a beautiful place both in its natural scenery and its buildings. Street after street of handsome residences, not apartment houses, lovely parks and the University of California with its numbers of buildings and wide beautiful drives and walks. I went all around and through them and then to see the "Greek Theater." This is an outdoor theater, built on the hillside which forms a natural amphitheater. It is built exactly like an old Greek theater and is the only copy of it in existence today. The stage and dressing rooms are a stone building at the foot of the hills, or rather the dressing rooms are the building and the stage is a cement platform with no roof. There are large stone columns in the front of the dressing rooms, dividing the opening on the stage. The center circle before the stage is a sawdust ring for wrestling matches, etc., and the seats rise one above the other like a grandstand only in a semicircle up the sides of the hills, which completely surround them and rise above the highest seat like a rampart, completely around the seats, with tall pine trees growing on the top. There is no roof but the blue sky and the whole thing is very wonderful and beautiful besides being world famous.

We climbed the hill behind the Greek Theater and ate our lunch with Oakland, Berkeley, the blue bay and the city of San Francisco spread at our feet, with still more hills or mountains rising at our backs and a blue, blue sky above us. And this was beautiful Berkeley, "the city of homes."

After lunch we wandered down among the paths of the University grounds and so to the car line which we took to Oakland, and so home across the bay from another pier and on another steamer. From Berkeley to Oakland, you know, is following around the shore of the bay, although we were out of sight of it because of the houses. There is no space between the two—they are really one city and it is impossible to tell where the one ends and the other begins. It is wonderful to cross the bay at night out at the front of the boat near the water and I would never get tired of seeing the lights of San Francisco as the boat comes in. The ferry tower is very tall and all a mass of electric lights, and across it are the words in electric lights, "San Francisco invites the World—Panama-Pacific Exposition 1915," and then there are all the other electric lights and signs. I am getting so I can find my way around a little and even cross Market Street among the jitneys without being frightened.

Rose gave a little tea party for me yesterday, just a few of the girls and women who work on the *Bulletin* and who write. If you should see on the Margin of Life page a series of little stories, "The People in Our Apartment House," you may read them knowing that they are *true*. Rose is writing them and the "little artist girl who lives in the basement"* makes the pictures. I like Rose's women friends very much. The men at the *Bulletin* office are only acquaintances. Some of them are very pleasant to meet and some I dislike very much. Did I tell you that the Pelkie who was doing the artist work on the paper when I was at home has disappeared and there is a suspicion around the office that he was in

*Later to become the renowned Berta Hader, author-illustrator (with her husband) of children's books.

225

The Ferry Tower's huge "1915" greeted streetcar riders. Once aboard the ferries, they could read the Tower's other message, SAN FRANCISCO INVITES THE WORLD . . . PANAMA-PACIFIC EXPOSITION 1915.

some way connected with the German spy system here?

Yesterday after the 4 P.M. tea party we went down to the ferry to see Gillette's brother Edson start home. He came out unexpectedly and was in the city only one day on business so all we saw of him was a little while at the ferry station.

I love a ride on the streetcars at night and to get to the ferry station we go through the famous Barbary Coast. Most of the buildings on the street are closed and dark now, but a little nearer the station is what they call the "waterfront," where every building on the street is a saloon. Gillette says the sailors come ashore there with all their pay from a six-months' voyage and they have to have some place to get rid of their money. He says that if they have not managed to spend it all by two or three o'clock in the morning someone will obligingly hit them over the head with a piece of gaspipe and take it away from them.

I am glad Mr. Nall came back and that you are going to cement the rats and mice out. What an awful lot of rain you are having. I should think it would make the fall feed good. Here every morning the fog is so thick it looks as though it would rain, but towards noon it clears away and the sun shines usually until towards night when the fog drifts in again from the ocean like smoke and everything is dull and gray again. Rose is very busy writing her story and I keep busy doing one thing and another. She expects to get it all written this week and then she will likely be able to have a few days to play and we will see Mill Valley and the battleship and have another day at the Fair. Of course I am enjoying the visit but I want to see you and Inky.

    Bessie

POSTCARD
(EXHIBIT PALACE, CARNATION MILK
CONDENSERY, PACIFIC
INTERNATIONAL EXPOSITION,
SAN FRANCISCO 1915)

September 29, 1915

Dear Manly,

I'll tell you all how they condense milk when I come. Was shown all over this very particularly.

    Bessie

~m~

San Francisco
September 29, 1915

Manly Dear,

I spent yesterday afternoon at the Exposition. Rose went out to see an engineer at the Southern Pacific exhibit to get some facts for her railroad story and as Gillette had the day off we both went along and wandered around while she was talking to him.

We saw the kangaroos and the wallabies at the Australian exhibit. One kangaroo was taking his afternoon nap in a bed he had scooped out in the sand. The sun was shining brightly and very hot on his bed in the center of the wire yard and he lay flat on his back with his legs all sticking straight up and slept. A lady kangaroo was making herself a bed in the sand and another one was eating mud. A wallaby was hopping around. It looks like the kangaroos, only smaller, and its fur was gray instead of yellowish-brown. The kangaroos looked just like pictures of them, only more so. Their front parts are so much smaller and out of proportion to their hind parts that they look ugly and they seem very awkward as they hop around.

The Australian exhibit was mostly wool and minerals. The New Zealand Building was near. Their exhibit was wood and woolen goods and moving pictures showing harvesting scenes, fishing scenes, surf bathing, loading of ships with oysters, hemp, wool, and cheeses for export. There was also a stock show showing their cattle and horses, in pictures I mean, and they were fine. Do you remember when we talked of going to New Zealand? I liked the pictures of the country very much.

We went through the France and Belgium Building but our time was limited. Rose and I are going through them again and I will write about them then. They are wonderful.

We met Rose in the Hawaiian Gardens in the Horticultural Building. They are a delightful combination of flowers and shrubs, and a large pavilion where Hawaiian coffee and pineapple juice and salad and other combinations of pineapple are served at little tables. There is a fountain in the center and water vines and shrubs and flowers around the fountain's rim. The fountain and a little space are enclosed with golden ropes and there are marble pedestals inside with canaries in cages on them. At one side is a balcony where a Hawaiian band plays and sings their native songs, which are lovely. The canaries have heard the music so long that at certain places they take up the tune and sing an accompaniment. It is beautiful. The waiters are Hawaiian men and girls and it's a delightful place to sit and rest, listen to the music and sip either coffee or delicious pineapple juice. In the gardens are all kinds of strange plants and flowers and gold fishes in rock tanks. There are the immense tree ferns, ferns with stems as large as the trunks of trees and growing as high, date palms and other curious things.

We went from here to the Food Products Building where everything eatable is made and sold. Too long for a letter. I'll have to tell you about it.*

Then we went to the Manufacturers' Building and there I saw something I'm sure will interest you. It was the "Keen Kutter" exhibit. In the center

---

*What she told Manly must have been similar to the article she wrote for the Missouri *Ruralist* that appears at the end of these letters, beginning on page 277.

of the space, which was nearly two hundred feet square, was a river and a waterfall. The waves were chains, the waterfall was chains on a windlass, and the broken water below the falls was chains. Everything about the exhibit was worked by electricity. The waves were rolling down and over the waterfall. The broken water was running away below and a ship, the steel hull of which was a huge knife, sailed across the river above the falls, and a great snake made of some shining cutlery stuff crawls across at the foot of the picture. Above this scene is an arch made of glistening spoons of different sizes. At the upper right-hand corner was a gigantic pocket knife with four blades that kept opening and shutting and at the upper left-hand corner was a row of seven blacksmiths standing each at his anvil with a different tool in his hand. At stated times first one and then another would beat the tool on the anvil with his hammer, sharpening it apparently. At the center top were two windmills made of ax blades continually turning. At each side of the center (the center was the waterfall) was a fountain with the long streams of spray made of wire and the water made of bits, such as you use with your brace. The upper part of the water was just medium-size bits and then there was a rim on the fountain and then a circle of larger bits. They were all turning in the direction of boring, so it looked as though they were water running down, striking the rim, and then running down again. The illusion was *good*. The name "Keen Kutter Cutlery" was written above the whole thing with shiny padlocks and the whole thing was in motion moved by electricity. It was very interesting and it was positively uncanny to see that huge pocket knife open and shut, open and shut, as though it were alive and moving itself.

To cap the day, as we came home on the street-car a man sat near us who was chewing gum. He wore a stiff hat pulled down tight on his head and every time he chewed, his hat moved up and down fully two inches, up and down, up and down, with perfect regularity as though he were worked by electricity.

Regards to Mr. Nall.

Lovingly,

Bessie

San Francisco
October 1, 1915

Manly Dear,

Rose gave me a ten-dollar gold piece last night. This makes $20 she has given me and makes $30 in gold I have to bring home with me. I have $5 in change which I expect I will have to spend to get me home—sleeping car berth, food, etc. I mentioned going home to Rose and she begged very hard for me to stay as long as my ticket will let me, which will be November 15. She said she would keep on making it up to me for my time if I would only stay. You see, she has given me $5 a week for the time I have been here.

I am wondering if I would not earn more toward paying off the debts if I stayed in that way, and if you could get the fall work done and things in shape for winter if I did. How about it? If I stay the month of October, you see, I would have $60 to bring home with me if nothing happens to Rose's job, and that would help a lot. But of course it would not pay to do it if it will make you lose the potato crop or the other crops or anything like that. You are the one to say, because it is you who are having the hard time and you know how things are there.

Gillette just missed getting a good job this week by about an hour. He is gone today to see if he can do anything on a real estate deal. If it works he will make $150 or $200. If not, he has lost his expenses. There are a good many newspaper men here out of jobs. Gillette thinks that it is perhaps because there are so many out here for the year to see the Fair. He says if he can get a little ahead, a couple of hundred dollars, he believes he will try for a job in St. Louis or Kansas City. Rose says she would like to work in St. Louis and be where she could run down home, but she has such a good job here that she can not afford to give it up until she has a little ahead or a good job for sure back there. She is putting a part of her salary in the savings bank every week, besides running the house and what she gives me and Gillette's expense while he is trying to get something. He gets extra work every once in awhile and when he draws his pay he turns it all over to Rose and then every day takes just enough for his streetcar fare, lunch down town, and cigars.

Lovingly,
Bessie

~~~⚬~~~

POSTCARD
(CARNATION STOCK FARM.
ONE OF THE DAIRY FARMS WHICH SUPPLIED
FRESH MILK TO CONDENSERIES TO BE
EVAPORATED, STERILIZED AND HERMETICALLY
SEALED AS CARNATION MILK.)

October 4, 1915

Went to a "movie" theater last night that cost $600,000. Seats 4,000 people. Largest in U.S.

Lovingly, Bessie

~~~⚬~~~

San Francisco
October 4, 1915

Manly Dear,

I came home from down town by myself today. Rose's boss, managing editor, called her to come down to the office at twelve. She works at home, you know, and has been working very hard on a railroad story which was to begin in the Thursday paper. She has it nearly finished. I went down with her to see what was wanted and she thought that likely he wanted some little change made in the story.

236

What he wanted was that she should interview an Austrian musician who is giving concerts here. He is an international figure and a very wonderful player of the violin. He served four weeks in the Austrian army against the Russians and is wounded so that they will not have him any more. He has made some statements to the papers to the effect that there will be nothing worthwhile left in Europe when the war is over unless something is done to save a little from the wreck.

The money he gets for his playing is to be used for the artists in Europe (of whatever nationality) who need help to keep them alive. He says they are dying of starvation after they come out of the army as he has. He and his wife have adopted forty-three soldiers' orphans and are going to feed, clothe, and educate them as though they were truly their own.

Well, Rose's boss told her to go see him and get a story of his life and have it ready to start Thursday in place of the one she has been writing. They will publish the one she has been at work on later. This means that she will have to write it in a hurry, just ahead of the press.

So she went to interview the man and I came home.

There is a house part way down the hill where we live, the materials for which were brought around the Horn in the old days. The man who built it and his wife lived there until they were old and then they quarreled and the man deeded the wife half the house and lot, and had the house cut straight down through the middle and moved his half over onto his half of the lot and they lived there until they died. The house is up on the hill from the street.

A high rock wall runs along the street and in it is an iron gate. When one goes in the gate, he goes up four stone steps then turns and goes up a flight of stone steps. These steps are all inside the stone wall. Solid stone is on each side and overhead. At the top of these stone stairs one comes out into the outdoors on a stone walk. From here one can go around the head of the stairs on a little stone balustrade and out on a little stone balcony overhanging the street, or turn the other way, go up some broad deep stone steps for a little way, then up some more stone stairs and then some wooden stairs to the front door of the house. From the front room of the house there is a view over the tops of the houses and out on the bay. The little artist girl [Berta] who illustrated some of my verses has rented the front part of the house and is moving in. I love to go there just for the sake of going up those stone stairs inside the stone wall.

There was a little earthquake shock here Saturday night, or at least the paper said so the next morning. I did not feel it. It reached all up and down the coast and was heaviest in Nevada.

You surely must have got my letter by this time in which I told you about going out on the boat to see the sunset, but it will bear telling again. It was a small white launch and it cost fifty cents each. We were gone an hour. It started from the anchorage inside the fairgrounds and headed straight out for the Golden Gate where the sun was going down. Rose and I stayed on deck and right in the very front of the boat, where we saw only the rail and the few feet of deck in front of us and the rest was water. We kept one hand on a rope to steady ourselves and stood our feet a little wide apart and there we stood and faced the wind and the sun and the fog streaming in and felt the sway and pitch of the boat under our feet. Oh, it was delightful when we met the ocean swell near the Gate.

We went past the Exposition grounds and then

An Alaska Packers schooner in the Golden Gate, as Laura saw it. The bridge was built there twenty years later.

the Presidio headlands to the Golden Gate and reached there just as the sun dipped out of sight. Then we turned and came around to come back on the other side of the bay, past the highest fort in the world and we knew that the huge disappearing guns were lurking there, past the buildings of the fort around the base of the mountain and the lighthouse out on the point of rock, past Angel Island where the quarantine station is, and then headed back across the bay for the anchorage. The fog closed in around us so that we were out of sight of land, sailing over a gray sea with the gray fog walling us in. The wind was driving the spray and fog in my face and the boat would rise and swoop and fall under my feet and it was glorious. Going on a ferry boat is not nearly so much fun, for the boat is so much larger that it rides steadier.

I am so glad Mr. Nall is with you and that you are getting the corn and peas taken care of, and so much of the other work done. Give my regards to Mr. Nall.

Lovingly,
Bessie

PRIVATE:*

Gillette has a job on the *Call* for a week now, so he will feel better. I tell you, this being in a city and out of a job is no fun.

Rose has syndicated† her Charlie Chaplin story. The syndicate is to take all the expense and trouble of selling to papers and magazines and Rose gets half the selling price. They tell her that they think they can sell it to papers in small towns and get an income from it of $500 a week for five weeks. The story runs for five weeks, you know, and the papers pay for it as they use it, at so much a week. Rose thinks that they are seeing things larger than they will turn out but she hopes to get something from it.

The more I see of how Rose works the better satisfied I am to raise chickens. I intend to try to do some writing that will count, but I would not be

---

*In the original this is a separate piece of paper. Laura probably expected that Almanzo would read many of her letters aloud to friends in Mansfield, and she wanted to make sure this was not read.

†A syndicator offered a story written for a single newspaper to hundreds of papers all over the country for republication at a relatively small price to each.

driven by the work as she is for anything and I do not see how she can stand it.

Lovingly,

Bessie

———ɯ———

San Francisco
October 6, 1915

Manly Dear,

My last letter, you remember, was written when I had come home from down town by myself. Well, the funniest thing happened. When I came home, before I wrote you, I ran down to see the little artist girl. I was afraid Rose might come home while I was gone and be worried if I was not here, so I left a note for her saying where I was. When I came home from Berta's I carelessly left the note on the table and went on into my bedroom and wrote my letter to you on the typewriter. Well, Rose was worried about my coming home by myself, so when it was time that I should have arrived she phoned to me from down town. Being at Berta's I, of course, did not answer, and they [the telephone operators] reported that they could not get me.

She finished her interview with Fritz Kreisler

and went back to finish her business at the *Bulletin* office and as soon as she got there phoned again. Still no answer. She was worried, but had to go see the City Editor, and while she was in his office one of the girls in Miss Beatty's office kept trying to get me. Rose came down and the girl told her she could not get me, and Rose was terror-stricken and came rushing home as fast as the streetcar could bring her. All the way she kept thinking that an automobile had killed me—and remembering that I had nothing with me that would identify me, for I had not taken my purse. She rushed through the door thinking that she would phone the emergency hospital, and there on the table was my note saying I had gone to Berta's. She did not stop long enough to hear the typewriter clicking in the bedroom but rushed out again and down to Berta's. Berta said I had been gone for three quarters of an hour, so she ran to Bessie Beatty's across the street. I was not there. Then Rose hurried to the little grocery where she buys her things, which was quite a little way, but I had not been there, so she rushed home again and while crossing the room to telephone the police she heard the typewriter and found me peacefully writing my letter to you.

I told her she should have thought I would find

my way home somehow, but she was afraid I had been in an accident. She says that every day someone, and usually more are run over by the automobiles, and said she would never let me out of her sight again. But nevertheless I went down town and back again by myself yesterday and I had to cross Market Street to get to the *Bulletin* office, and that is the worst street in the city. I had no trouble.

We have had the thickest fog ever for several days. All night and all day we can hear the sirens on the different islands and headlands, and the ferries and ships at anchor in the bay keep their foghorns bellowing. We can not see the bay at all nor any part of San Francisco except the few close houses on Russian Hill. The foghorns sound so mournful and distressed, like lost souls calling to each other through the void. (Of course, no one ever heard a lost soul calling, but that's the way it sounds.) It looks as though Russian Hill were afloat in a gray sea and Rose and I have taken the fancy that it is loosened from the rest of the land and floating across the sea to Japan. That is the feeling it gives one.

There are eight big ocean-going ships outside the Golden Gate that can not find their way in through the fog and are waiting for it to clear. One is a passenger ship from the Orient, one is a U.S. transport, one is a Greek tramp. The rest are passenger ships from the coast cities and one of them is filled with passengers and crew from a wrecked and abandoned ship. There they all are, so close to land and can't get in.

I must tell you about Rose's interview with Fritz Kreisler, the Austrian violinist who served four weeks in the trenches and came out wounded so that he is unfit for further service. I think I wrote you that he was sending all he could make back to help, not to carry on the war, but to save other artists from starving and to care for those forty-three children they have adopted.

He said there was no hatred for each other among the soldiers and that all these stories of barbarities committed by the soldiers of one side on the wounded of the other side were simply made up by the papers and those higher up for the sake of inflaming popular passion and creating a hatred. He said that both German and Russian, when gathering up the wounded from a battlefield, took them all, German and Russian, and treated them alike.

Among the children they are supporting are

three Russian families. Mrs. Kreisler was a nurse with the Austrian army. He says she was so tender-hearted that when a wounded soldier could not die in peace for worrying about his children she would promise him that if Mr. Kreisler lived to come back they would take care of them. When he came back she had promised forty-three, among them were the three Russian soldiers.

He said that in one battle where the Austrians retreated the Russians gathered up among the wounded an Austrian with a shattered jaw. They fixed his wound as well as possible but he could not eat solid food. In the company were a few eggs and they fed them all to this wounded Austrian and went without themselves, not knowing how soon they would need them. Mr. Kreisler came to know about it because a few days later the Austrians charged and recaptured the place, and the wounded Austrian told them. This too when the Russians did not have enough of anything to eat. Remember that it is an Austrian telling this story of the Russians. Rose says both Fritz Kreisler and his wife are the loveliest people she has ever met.

We are going to the Greek Theater tomorrow to hear him play.

Eggs are fifty cents a dozen here now.

Take good care of yourself and Inky. I am anxious to get an answer to my letter in which I asked you to say how long I might stay. If I stay until my ticket expires which will be November 15, Rose will be able to take the ocean trip with me to Los Angeles. If I do not stay until that time I will have to give up seeing Los Angeles and the ocean trip and come home as my ticket reads.

Lovingly,
Bessie

———

San Francisco
October 14, 1915

Manly Dear,

It has been several days since I wrote you so I will begin back where I left off.

Rose and I went over to Berkeley to hear Fritz Kreisler, the Austrian, play the violin. This you know meant a trip across the bay, which is always such a pleasure, then a streetcar ride through Oakland, for this time we landed at the Oakland pier, then a walk across the campus or college grounds to the Greek Theater which I have described to you before.

It was wonderfully beautiful at night. The lights were lit until the people were seated and when the concert began they were all turned off except the lights on the stage. The stage and the walls behind, like the wings of a theater, are white marble and the tops of the tall pines and eucalyptus trees showed above it. The hills rise around the amphitheater so that the seats as they rise one above the other have the solid hillside behind them. The hills rise still higher than the seats with the large trees growing on them, so as we sat in the theater the trees rose all around above us. The moon shone just above the stage and it was all so beautiful that when Kreisler's violin began to sing it made one's throat ache. There was a complete orchestra of stringed instruments to play the accompaniments to Kreisler. The music was the most beautiful I have ever heard. We sat for two hours, almost without breathing, listening to it. The seats were crowded and all we could see of the people was a dark blur and all the white faces. They were all as still and listening as intently as we were.

Then there was the ride home across the bay and by streetcar. We got home at one o'clock and were very tired. But, oh, the next day we were so stiff from sitting on those cold, hard rock seats for so long that we could hardly move. My tiredness settled in my eyes and I haven't been able to use them much since. Did I tell you I got a pair of as-good-as-gold-trimmed just plain magnifying glasses at the ten-cent store here? They help so much. I could not read or write without them but my eyes get so tired even when I use them that I'm afraid the man in Springfield was right and they need particular ones.

Oh, the other day as Rose and I walked down town we saw in the window of an antique shop a silver watch that weighs three pounds. It was made for a prospector from the very first silver ever mined in California. It was made in 1848. Beside it was a tray of small, beautiful, beautiful jeweled watches made in the 16th century (400 years ago) in France.

Sunday about five o'clock Rose finished writing for the day and she and I took a streetcar for the ocean beach. We got off at Land's End and walked around by the shore to the Cliff House. We watched the waters awhile from the Cliff House balcony and then went down to the edge of the water on the shore where the waves could roll in at our feet and watched the beautiful colors of sunset fade away from sea and sky and the dark come over the waters. I do love the ocean so much—the sight of it and the sound of it and the smell of it.

Tuesday Rose and I spent all day at the Fair. She let me plan the day as I wished, so we went down early—got to the grounds about 9:30.

First we looked at the kangaroos and wallabies. They are in a wire yard between the Australian and New Zealand Buildings. From there we went through the Australian Building and found there the most wonderful exhibit of native woods we have seen yet. I did not know that such beautiful woods grew anywhere and I did so wish you and Mr. Nall could see them.* They show each kind of wood in the rough, in slabs and timbers and planks. Then they have each kind finished and polished naturally, and then they have furniture made of each kind. Myrtle wood was the loveliest. There was a bedroom set of it. Price $2,000.00. Then there are different kinds of oak, among them the "silky oak" that looks just like watered silk. There are different kinds of pine and ever so many

*Almanzo was an accomplished cabinetmaker and carpenter. A number of his creations are on display today at the Wilder home in Mansfield. Laura knew he would be interested in wood varieties as well as woodworking tools.

others. The hard woods of Australia are almost fireproof, and there are on exhibition some timbers that have been under water for thirty years, still sound. There were all kinds of grains and strange fruits and vegetables and mountains of wool and metals and minerals. We met a couple of Australian newspaper men, "press men," as they call them, and they told us a good deal about Australia and gave us a lot of literature which I will bring home. One of them was *Captain* somebody. He wore a fierce little mustache, waxed and twisted so tight that it stood straight out and he had the scar of an old saber cut across the corner of his mouth.

From Australia we went to France, which is just across the street. It is a large white marble palace and there we stayed for two hours and a half, walking and looking all the time and it seemed only a few minutes. There are lovely gowns and hats and shoes and gloves for women, men's shirts and shoes and gloves and suspenders, the most beautiful fabrics (cloth of different kinds) that could be imagined. There are world-famous paintings and statues. There are wonderful old tapestries, each of which covers an entire wall. Rose and I estimated that some of the larger ones were fifty by seventy-five feet. Imagine a picture of that size drawn by a famous artist and then woven thread by thread of the most beautiful colors in the softest tones and all mellowed by time. They are most wonderful. The coloring of the flesh of people, the colors in the sky, and trees and grass, horses, birds and beasts, water and land, all perfect and never fading. Some of them were made in Brussels, the capital in Belgium, that the Germans have now. There was an old hand-carved and gilded bedstead and the body of an old carriage made 500 years ago when Louis XIV was king of France. There were wonderfully made cabinets of brass inlaid with silver and beautiful old furniture and carpets made for Louis XIV. I can not tell you of all but I am bringing a catalog and I will go over it with you.

I think they have paid a fine compliment to the U.S. in some of their exhibits. They have a bronze statue of the "Minute Man of 1776," the American revolutionary soldier, you know. I recognized him the minute I saw him, and nearby there is a small booth filled with personal belongings of General Lafayette, who fought with Washington, you remember. There is a desk and chair he used to use, a couple of his swords crossed, a lamp and inkhorn, his very own old cocked hat that he used to wear and it looks exactly like the pictures we used to see. There is a portrait of him, and one of General Washington and the other French general who helped us.

Oh, I must tell you of the wonderful ropes and strings of pearls, white and pink and black. Then there were some individual pearls, both white and black, as large as a quail's egg.*

There is one little long room. As we came to the archway opening into it and looked down we saw on each side large paintings of battle scenes where the French and Germans were fighting in the old war. There were cities burning, with men fighting in the streets. Generals on horseback leading the cavalry in. Pictures of this kind were on all the length of the walls until near the farther end. There, on each side, was a painting of Christ crucified, the only pictures of the kind I ever saw that were not horrible. These were wonderful. Between them in the center of the room was a bronze statue of Sorrow, a woman weeping. The most realistic thing. It almost made me cry to look at it. At the end of the room, covering the whole end wall with the Christ on each side and the weeping

* About three fourths of an inch long.

woman before it, was a painting of the armies of France. It was a camp at night with a little sentinel fire at one side. The rifles were stacked in a long row down the picture, growing smaller and smaller in the distance. The flag was rolled and resting across the tops of the rifles nearby and the soldiers all lay wrapped in their blankets sleeping. Dawn was just breaking along the skyline and on the clouds rolling away rode the "Phantom Armies of France," the ghosts, I think, of all men and horses who have ever been killed in all the wars of France. The whole picture was the most wonderful lifelike thing I have ever seen and the whole room was a shrine of sorrow.

From France we went to Belgium, which is an annex of the French Building and filled with what poor Belgium could gather up from the wreck. There is a relief map, a model of the city of Brussels, and some beautiful old paintings, and the statues of King Albert and Queen Elizabeth in white marble, looking exactly like those good pictures of them we have in the Metropolitan. After we saw Belgium we went to the Food Products Building, got a couple of Scotch scones and then went to the East Indian tea room in the same building and got some tea and cakes to eat with the scones and sat and rested a few minutes.

Then we went back and after taking another look at the kangaroos we went into the New Zealand Building where they show moving pictures of the country and people. Do you remember when we had a notion of going to New Zealand before we went to Florida? It is surely a great country. The pictures showed harvesting grain in the hills, too rough for machinery, cut with a sickle, bound by hand and threshed with a flail. They showed a harvest where the ground is just a gentle rolling country. There were four harvesters in the field and the grain was fine. The grain was hauled from the field and threshed before our eyes.

We saw also the loading on ships at the docks of oysters, hemp, cheese, wool, and frozen mutton. There were pictures of the great sheep herds and the sheep dogs and shepherds and hundreds and hundreds of sheep. We saw them made to swim through the tanks and we saw them sheared. Also we saw the native islanders that used to be the cannibal tribes in Australia and New Zealand. We saw also the hot-water lake and the steaming cliffs. Believe me, I would stay far from it. The high rock cliffs are pouring hot water into the hot lake from springs all around it and wherever the springs come out of the rocks or the water splashes on them clouds of steam rise. A boat loaded with people went out on the hot-water lake amidst the steam and went around it. The water was so hot they could not put their hands in—one tried and burned himself. There were the hot springs and geysers in another place too, and then pictures of surf bathing on the ocean beach where the people stood away out with boards in their hands and as the waves came in dropped down and rode their boards in.

When we were through here we went down to the Marina, which is the walk along the shore, and saw the gray battleships and the ferries and the ships and boats they were trimming up for the landing of Columbus in the evening, and then home through the lovely courts to an entrance gate where we took the streetcar. We were too late to go out to the battleship as we had intended and so that is left for the next day.

Why! I told you why I changed the address. Mail that comes to the *Bulletin* for us is sent upstairs to Bessie Beatty's office and thrown down on a desk among a pile of papers and there are five

Fisherman's Wharf as it looked shortly after Laura's visit.

careless people there to paw it over, and I did not get your letter enclosing the one from Wilhelm, so I sent you the house address where we live which is 1019 B. Vallejo St., San Francisco.

Lovingly,
Bessie

—⁓⁓—

Rose wrote a note to Almanzo which she enclosed with her mother's letter of October 14.

Papa Dear—

Something is happening which I think you should know, though to me, especially, it is a painful subject to contemplate. I notice Mama Bess says nothing about it in her letters, but I can quite understand why she does not. Still, I feel it is only right you should know, and think it my duty to tell you.

Mama Bess is growing fat.

I do not know whether or not it is the fish she eats. She eats a tremendous amount of it. Yet, fish is supposed to be good brain food. I never heard that it was fattening.

Perhaps it is the Scotch scones. They are very delicious, crumbly, hot cakes, spread thick with butter and jam. She eats two of them without a quiver. Once she ate three. Afterward she said she felt queer, and wondered if she had eaten something. It may be the scones.

I will not take her to the scone booth again. It is always a dangerous undertaking anyway, because it is just beside the fish exhibit, and she stands outside the glass cases, looking at the trout and salmon and rock cod and flounders and sand dabs and catfish and ratfish and crabs and shrimps and sea cucumbers and sole, and I am in mortal terror every minute that she will not be able to restrain herself any longer, but will break the glass and eat some of them right there. Even with two scones and a package of Pan-pak and fifteen cents worth of salted nuts and a rosecake and a bag of Saratoga chips in her hand, she still looks at the fish with the same longing expression.

No, I shall not take her to the scone booth any more. I shall go myself, and bring the scones out. Or leave her standing by the big guns where they pop the rice. Ever eat popped rice? It's better than popcorn. Gillette eats it with butter and salt, the same way.

Mama Bess has just interrupted—I am supposed to be writing the "Behind the Headlights" story—she has just interrupted and said, "Luncheon is served." When she cooks the luncheon it's so delicious you can't help overeating. I fear by the time you get this she will be still fatter.

Anyway, I've done my duty and told you.

Lots of Love,

Rose

—⟋⟍⟍⟍—

And then Rose had to write again.

San Francisco
October 20, 1915

Dear Papa—

I meant to write you sooner, and hope you have not been worried by not getting a letter from Mama Bess. She was hurt by a streetcar last week but is all right now. She does not want anyone in Mansfield to know about it, because she says it looks as if she could not take care of herself in a city, but on account of not writing for so long she thought I had better write and tell you.

It was not her fault at all. She was going down town with Gillette, and he jumped off the car while it was going full speed. She stood up suddenly, surprised by the way he did, and fell off. The back of her head struck the stone pavement, and things looked pretty bad for awhile, but they got her to a hospital right away and the doctor said there was no danger, it was only a superficial wound, no fracture or anything like that. She is coming home today.

It has been too bad, because she has lost a

The running boards on this streetcar make it easy to see how Laura fell.

Market Street, which Laura crossed to get to the Bulletin *office, located on the far side just to the right of the lamppost in the foreground.*

263

whole week and it will probably be another before she can get around and see much. We will not be able to get anything from the streetcar company because it was not their fault at all.

She has been in the best hospital in town, and except for a bad headache she has been quite comfortable. Of course she is pretty weak yet, from the shock and all, but that will be gone in a few days more. She had written you a long letter, and had it in her hand when the accident occurred. We can not find it, and suppose it has been mailed to you all right by someone who picked it up. It had a note in it from me, so you will know by that whether or not you got it.

She has an order for several articles from the [Missouri] *Ruralist*, and she will get them this next week and we will write them up. That will be some real money for her.

I did not read her your first letter about not being well until the second came that said you were better. I hope you're feeling fine by this time; when I read the first letter I certainly felt blue.

She told me what to tell you to feed the hens, and I wrote it down on a sheet of hospital paper. I will send it with this.

She says she supposes there is no use feeding

them much if they are getting so much corn, she says probably that is the reason they are not laying, because they get too much corn, which is not good to make them lay, and they have so much of that they do not eat things that would make them lay.

It certainly has been too bad, that she was needed at home so much. She is always worrying about how you are getting along and it is a shame I could not have had a little more money so you could have a man and someone to cook for you, both. But I suppose even then you would not find her cooking as good as yours by a long ways.

I am writing the life of Henry Ford* now, and he was telling me yesterday that he is building a farm tractor now that sells for $200 and weighs only 1,500 pounds. It runs for eleven hours on fifty-four cents worth of kerosene. It is not on the market yet, but will be, soon, and it struck me it would be better than a team of horses for lots of the farm work, because it would not cost any more, and when it was not working it would not be eating, and you could make it go fast or slow just as you liked. I am going to ask him more about it.

*The story was part of a series for the *Bulletin*. In 1917 it was published in book form as *Henry Ford's Own Story*, as told to Rose Wilder Lane.

I am going down to the hospital now to get Mama Bess and bring her out to the house. She said to tell you, whatever you did, to take good care of yourself and Inky till she gets back. She says she thinks she ought to start pretty soon, on account of your being there with all the work to do, but my private opinion is that she's homesick. I want her to see a little more of the state, Petaluma, and some of Marin County, though, before she leaves. It is hard to show her as much as I would like to because I have to keep on earning my little pay envelope, and that takes a lot of time.

Lots and lots of love,

Rose

ENCLOSURE:

Mama says, about the hens—if you have not already mixed up the package of fenugreek* that is on the end of the long shelves near the woodshed door—mix it up with the package of cayenne pepper that is on the shelf beside it, and the same quantity of ginger, then add lime until it is the right color—she says you know what color it should be.

---

*An herb used in livestock feed.

Feed it the same as Pratts food—about two tablespoons to a dishpan of feed.

For their morning mess feed them as much mash as they will eat up *clean* in twenty minutes— don't feed them any more than that.

Recipe for morning mash:
4 measures bran
2 measures corn chop (fine ground chop is
    best)
1 measure cut bone
¹/₂ measure linseed meal
If you think they need more lime, put more in
    the feed—maybe a couple of tablespoons
    in a feed. And do not forget the salt.

<hr>

San Francisco
October 22, 1915

Manly Dear,

I am so sorry you have been sick and that Inky hurt himself. Rose says she wrote you that I got hurt. I am all right, only a little weak yet. I had thought by this time I would have everything done and be ready to start home. I know I should be there helping you get things ready for winter unless by some good chance you were making things ready without me, but I might have known that you would not be able to get help if you particularly wanted it.

At last I have a letter from the *Ruralist* with orders for copy and recommendations that give me passes into the Fair and throws the whole Missouri part of it wide open to me. It is a shame they could not have sent it sooner and I do not understand why they did not. The men in charge of the Missouri exhibits want me to persuade the *Ruralist* to issue a special edition on Missouri at the P.P.I.E. [Panama Pacific International Exposition] and I have wired them about it. If they tell me to go ahead with it I will have my hands full for a few days getting out the copy for the whole paper. I expect to hear from them tomorrow. If I do the special edition I will not be able to start for home before ten days, but if I just write the articles I already have the orders for I expect to start for home in a week from now.*

---

*Laura did write the lead story for a spread on the Missouri exhibits at the Fair, which appeared the day after the P.P.I.E. closed—December 5, 1915. And she wrote another article about food at the Fair, with recipes, which is condensed at the end of these letters, beginning on p. 277.

I have given up the idea of the ocean trip. It would break into Rose's work and she is very busy. I would not care to go alone and it would cost more than to come straight home. So I will take the train here for Kansas City without change. I am also going to let the trip to Petaluma go. I would rather spend the time at the Fair, save the expense and the tiresome train ride, and get all the information I want from the experts at the poultry exhibit here.

So you see I have mapped out for myself the work for the *Ruralist*, a couple of Sunday stories for the [St. Louis] *Post Dispatch*, learning what I can at the poultry exhibit here, a day on the battle-ship *Oregon* already arranged for, and then home. Perhaps you think it has taken me longer than it should have to make my visit but you have no idea how confusing this great city of San Francisco was to me and how a very little of the crowds and the streets tired me. Rose has been very busy too and because of that we could not always do as we would have liked to do.

I have accomplished some of the things that I came to do to my entire satisfaction and some are still up in the air. Stine has been out of town ever since I have been here so that we have been unable to find out anything definite about that $250 or any more to stop [mortgage] interest with, but Rose will try again within a day or two. I did so want to bring it home with me but if I can not do that it will come later. Gillette is working extra now with fair prospect of a regular job next week. If he gets it things will be smoothed out considerably.

Rose got into the movies again, unknown to her until it was all over. She was taken with the Henry Ford party on board the battleship *Oregon*. She is working now on the life of Ford, which will begin soon in the *Bulletin*. I do not know whether the outlaw story will be published in book form or not. If you are reading Rose's story of the engineer you may like to know that every incident in it is true. She went all around hunting up engineers to talk with and she found one that fired on an engine through Dakota north of us during the long winter,* or rather did not fire, because the trains could not run. In that part of the story Rose used some of what he told her and some that I told her.

Rose and Gillette are out chasing around after Ford to get more material for Rose's story (it being

---

*See *The Long Winter*, which Laura wrote over twenty years later, about her girlhood in De Smet, Dakota (now South Dakota).

Sunday Gillette is not working). I would be with them, only I am not quite strong enough yet. I am going to the Fair tomorrow and do some of the Missouri work in a motor chair like the one they pictured Steve with once.

Oh, I know Millman, who draws Steve. He is a fine young fellow, red-headed and with a funny quirk to the corner of his lips when he smiles and simply delightful in a clean, wholesome way. To show his sympathy for me because I got hurt he is going to give me an original drawing of Steve—the pen and ink picture that he made himself and that the pictures in the paper are made from.

Do take care of yourself and Inky and whisper to him that I will be there before long. I have so many nice things planned to do when I do get home and I am sure the woods are beautiful. I love the city of San Francisco. It is beautiful but I would not give one Ozark hill for all the rest of the state that I have seen. Oh, by the way, Missouri has SHOWN THEM* at the P.P.I.E. Carried off more prizes than any state except California and beat California on mines.

*Missouri is known as the "Show Me" State.

271

The Court of the
Universe from the
Tower of Jewels.
The Oregon, *where
Rose was photographed
with Henry Ford, is on
the left.*

The intricately carved wooden chest Laura brought home with her from the Fair, now in the Laura Ingalls Wilder Museum in Mansfield, Missouri.

Laura and Gillette sightseeing in the Muir Woods during her visit to San Francisco.

Do not expect to get any more long letters from me for I will be so busy doing all the writing I can for the papers and getting things wound up so I can start home that I will not have time. Nor do I think I should spend the time writing when I can be seeing more things and tell you about them all when I come.

I must stop now and rest a little for I am tired.
Goodbye for this time,
Lovingly, Bessie

Magic in Plain Foods

An article (condensed) by Laura which appeared in the [Missouri] Ruralist *on November 20, 1915.*

The thought came to me, while I wandered among the exhibits in the Food Products Building at the San Francisco Exposition, that Aladdin with his wonderful lamp had no more power than the modern woman in her kitchen. She takes down the receiver to telephone her grocery order, and immediately all over the world the monstrous genii of machinery are obedient to her command. All the nations of the world bring their offerings to her door—fruits from South America, Hawaii, Africa; tea and spices from India, China and Japan; olives and oil from Italy; coffee from strange tropical islands; sugar from Cuba and the Philippines.

This modern magic works both ways. The natives of all these far away places may eat the flour made from the wheat growing in the fields outside our kitchen windows. I never shall look at Missouri wheat fields again without thinking of the "Breads of All Nations" exhibit, where natives of eight foreign nations, in the national costumes, were busy making the breads of their countries from our own American flour.

We use raisins, flour, tea, breakfast food, and a score of other common things without a thought of the modern miracles that make it possible for us to have them.

One has a greater feeling of respect for the flour used daily, after seeing the infinite pains taken to turn out the perfect article. From the time the wheat is poured into the hoppers until, in our kitchens, we cut the string that ties the sack, the flour is not exposed to the outer air. It is not touched by human hands until we dip the flour sifter into it.

Ten years ago, too, we seeded our raisins by hand ourselves, or bribed the children to the task by giving them a share to eat. Today we buy seeded raisins in boxes, without giving a thought to how the seeding is done. You may be sure of this—these package raisins are clean. They are scientifically clean, sterilized by steam and packed hot. In the

Food Products Building I saw these machines at work. This is the process:

Sun-dried Muscat grapes are stemmed by machinery, then sent through 26 feet of live steam at 212 pounds pressure. From this they fall onto a steel, sawtooth cylinder, and pass under three soft rubber rolls which crush the raisin and loosen the seeds. They then strike a corrugated steel roll which throws out the seeds. The raisin passes on, is lifted from the cylinder by a steel rake and dropped into paraffin-paper-lined boxes, which are closed while the raisins are still hot from the steam sterilizing.

Space forbids that I should describe the scores of exhibits in this enormous [Food Products] building devoted to the preparation of different foods, a task which always has been considered woman's work. I can only briefly mention the Japanese rice cakes—tiny bits of paste half an inch long and no thicker than paper. The smiling Oriental in charge drops them into boiling olive oil, and they puff into delicious looking brown rolls three inches long. They look as toothsome as a homemade doughnut, but to your wild amazement, when you bite them there is nothing there.

I must say one word about the rose cakes:

delicious cakes baked in the form of a rose, and as good as they are beautiful. And I am sure nobody leaves the Exposition without speaking of the Scotch scones; everybody eats them who can reach them. They are baked by a Scotchman from Edinburgh, who turns out more than 4,000 of them daily. They are buttered, spread with jam, and handed over the counter as fast as four girls can do it. And the counter is surrounded by a surging mob all day long.

As I went from booth to booth, they gave me samples of the breads they had made, with our American flour—the little, bland Chinese girl in her bright blue pajama costume, the smiling high-cheeked Russian peasant girl, the Hindoo in his gay turban, the swarthy, black-eyed Mexican—all of them eager to have me like their national foods. And I must say I did like most of it so well that I brought the recipes away with me, and pass them on to you:

Russian Forrest

One pound flour, yolks of 3 eggs, 1 whole egg, 1/2 cup milk. Mix well and knead very thoroughly. Cut in pieces size of walnuts; roll very, very thin. Cut the center in strips, braid together and fry in deep fat. Drain, and sprinkle with powdered sugar.

Mexican Tamale Loaf

One pound veal, 1 onion, 2 cloves of garlic, 1 tablespoon chili powder, 1 can tomatoes (strained), 24 green olives (chopped). Boil the meat until very tender, take from the broth, cool and chop. Return to the broth, add salt to taste, add the onion and garlic chopped fine, then the tomatoes, olives and chili powder. Let all come to the boiling point, then add enough yellow cornmeal to make as thick as mush, turn into molds and set aside to cool. The loaf may be served either cold or sliced and fried.

German Honey Cake

One cup honey, molasses or syrup; ½ cup sugar, 2 cups flour, 1 teaspoon cinnamon, 1 teaspoon cloves, 1 teaspoon ginger, 2 teaspoons baking powder. Beat honey and sugar 20 minutes, then add the spices, the baking powder, and lastly the flour. Pour into well-buttered baking sheets and bake 15 minutes in a moderate oven. Cover with chocolate icing and cut in squares.

Italian White Tagliarini

Three cups flour, $^1/_2$ cup hot water, 2 eggs, 1 teaspoon salt. Mix and knead thoroughly, roll very thin as for noodles, and cut in any desired shape. Allow to dry 1 hour and cook in boiling water for 10 minutes, drain, and serve with sauce.

Sauce for Tagliarini

One-half cup olive oil, 1 large pod garlic, 1 large carrot, 1 large can tomatoes, salt and pepper, 2 large onions, 5 stalks celery, 1 cup parsley, $^1/_2$ pound hamburg steak, $^1/_8$ teaspoon cloves, $^1/_2$ cup butter. Heat the oil in an iron skillet or kettle, then add onions and garlic chopped fine. Cook until transparent but not brown, then add the rest of the ingredients chopped fine. Cook slowly for 2 hours.

Croissants (French Crescents)

Four cups flour, 1 cup warm water, 1 cake compressed yeast, $^1/_2$ teaspoon salt, 1 cup butter. Sift and measure the flour into a bowl, add the yeast which has been dissolved in the water, then the salt. Mix and knead thoroughly. Let rise 2 or 3 hours, then roll out 1 inch thick and lay the butter on the center. Fold the dough over and roll out four times as for puff paste, then cut in pieces as for finger rolls, having the ends thinner than the middles. Form in crescent shape, brush with egg, and bake in a moderate oven.

Chinese Almond Cakes

Four cups flour, 1 cup lard, $1^{1}/_{2}$ cups sugar, 1 egg, $^{1}/_{2}$ teaspoon baking powder. Mix and knead thoroughly. Take off pieces of dough the size of an English walnut, roll in a smooth round ball, then flatten about half. Make a depression on the top and place in it 1 almond. Place on pans, 2 inches apart, and bake a golden brown.

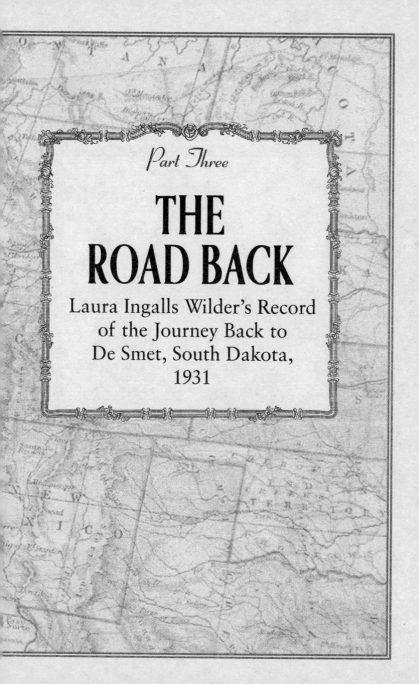

Part Three

THE
ROAD BACK

Laura Ingalls Wilder's Record
of the Journey Back to
De Smet, South Dakota,
1931

Introduction

Dear Reader:

My father, Roger Lea MacBride, was a teenager when he met Rose Wilder Lane. (His father introduced them. She was already a successful author.) In time they became close friends, and he later, as her attorney, handled her personal affairs and her estate. Rose told my father many wonderful stories about her parents, and through those stories both the real and the fictional Laura Ingalls Wilder came alive for me.

In 1931, sixty-four-year-old Laura Ingalls Wilder and her seventy-four-year-old husband, Almanzo, decided to reverse their 1894 journey and go back to De Smet, South Dakota, to the place where Laura's Ma and Pa had finally settled down. This was Laura and Almanzo's first trip home since they had left, almost forty years earlier, to seek a new life in Missouri, the Land of the Big Red Apple. Instead of a horse and wagon, they traveled by Buick.

The time was the Great Depression, and the area Laura and Almanzo traveled through was experiencing a severe drought. Always a keen observer of details, Laura made note of the prices of goods she and Almanzo bought and the condition of the towns they passed through. She also chronicled how things had changed in the years since she had moved away to Missouri. She wrote these notes to save, and even sent a batch of them home to her daughter, Rose, for safekeeping, with this note:

Manchester, June 12

Rose Dearest:

   Am sending you notes made along the way. Please keep them for me. Everything is fine, Nero good as can be. Both of us feeling well.

   We'll stay a few days longer, then go on to the Black Hills.

Lots of love, we'll write more later,
Mama Bess*

This is the first time Laura's notes from that journey have been published. Laura and Almanzo's trip came at a pivotal time in Laura's life. She had recently finished writing a book based on her early childhood in Wisconsin. The story would be published in the following year, 1932, by Harper & Brothers as *Little House in the Big Woods*, and would become so beloved that Laura would end up writing eight more Little House books, becoming an internationally acclaimed children's author. But for now, during this leisurely trip with Almanzo back to where they fell in love, she was observing details with her keen eye and revisiting the people and the places she had not seen in the forty years since she was the Laura of the Little House books.

Abigail MacBride, 2006

---

*Laura, whose middle name was Elizabeth, was called "Mama Bess" to avoid confusion with Almanzo's sister Laura.

The three travelers: Laura, Almanzo, and Nero around the time of their trip to De Smet.

Shady Side Camp,
86 miles West of Mansfield,
June 6, 1931

A very good day, but a bum lunch in Halltown. Nice camp house with garage attached in an oak grove. $1.50. Stopped at 2 P.M., a short drive for the first day. No food at this camp. Little kitchen handy.

EXPENSES
Gas	$ .65
Dinner	1.00
Cookies & Milk	.20
Tablet Pencil	.10
Camp	1.50
	$3.45

Eureka, Kansas, June 7

LEFT SHADY SIDE AT 7:30. Lots of nice camps on road. Leaving Carthage on the left, went north on 71. Left Lamar on the right and on to Camp Clark. Then west on 54 to Ft. Scott.

A little west of Ft. Scott we passed Biglow schoolhouse and recognized it as the schoolhouse we had passed and camped near 40 years ago as we drove by with the team from De Smet, South Dakota, to Mansfield, Missouri. The schoolhouse at that time was just finished, with shavings still around the door, and Rose and Paul and George Cooley played with them.

At Uniontown where we had lunch, we confirmed the fact that it was the same schoolhouse built 40 years ago.

Had a good meal at Uniontown, then still west on 54 through Iola and to Eureka. Are staying at Highland Cabin Camp. Everything very clean and sanitary. Cabin with garage attached, natural gas stove, electric [Text missing] in yard, charges $1.00 for us and the dog. Police dogs all around so Nero didn't have much run.

People from Indiana in a cabin on one side. People from Oklahoma in the other. Indiana brought over their supper scraps for Nero. Later I took them the Sunday picture papers for their kids. Oklahoma people very nice.

We came 277 miles. Good roads all the way. Not tired. Good bed, furnished own bedding.

A fraction over 20 miles on one gallon of gasoline average.

Crimson poppies planted and in bloom both sides of Highway 71 for some distance just as we left 60 to 71.

Some Osage Orange hedges all day.

Road signs changed. No "Don't pass cars on curves," but now and then, saw one saying "Drive on pavement."

EXPENSES

Gasoline	$1.38
Dinner & Doughnuts	.70
Paper	.20
Bread & Milk	.14
Cabin	1.00
	$3.42

~~~

June 8

OUT OF HIGHLANDS CAMP AT 6:30 A.M. On dandy smooth graveled road, 54 headed for El Dorado.

First sight of really big Kansas pastures. Ponds of water. Let Nero out for his exercise. Passed big Standard Oil tanks and miles of oil derricks. All silent because of overproduction. Eureka had 5,000 population during boom, now only 2,000. And the town looked it. Saw road go over the horizon hill. Eleven miles per hour by the speedometer.

Very few cattle in pastures. Not worth the pasture bills. Nearing El Dorado's enormous crude-oil tanks. Looks like acres of white oil tanks. Soil looks strange, so black and so deep, but not solid enough somehow. Roads fine and well marked. Dinner at Newton at 11:30 A.M. Good dinner at cafe on highway on a main street. 81 straight through town.

Wind from south blowing strong. Cool this morning so we wore our coats and left windows nearly closed. Afternoon hot as blazes. Wind hot at times. Darn the wind! Crops short in height and heads of grain about $3\frac{1}{2}$ inches long. Road sanded—coarse sand mixed with soil keeps the road smooth and fine. 1:35 sitting beside road waiting for engine to cool. A following, hot wind plays the devil with an engine.

Stopped at 4 P.M. at the best camp yet, clean and convenient natural gas stove. Just north of Salina brushed and cleaned and washed. Nice toilets and restrooms. Hot and cold shower bath. Water, gas, electric lights, baths and garage.

Saw great Osage Orange hedges all day.

Drove 166 miles.

EXPENSES

Cabin all	$1.25
Gas	1.02
Fan belt	.60
Dinner	1.35
Hamburg	.15
	$4.37

———~~———

Salina Camp, June 9
STARTED AT 5:30 A.M.

Everyone feeling fine, after a good cup of tea made on the little gas stove.

A nice, cool morning, cloudy.

Crops looking fine. Soon came to Saline River. Then queer, steep, round hills, standing almost straight up on the prairie without a bush or a tree but outcroppings of rock near the top.

Out of Saline County into Ottowa County, more hills, then over the Solomon River, timber on the banks. Passed through Bennington. Pretty place, great elm trees on both sides of street. Highway for ½ mile out on flat prairie country with clumps of trees here and there. Still in the land of the Osage Orange hedge. Prosperous-looking country. Nice farmhouses. Saw our first cottonwood trees. Nice house in grove of the trees that were at least 2 feet through. Wouldn't have thought I would have recognized the cottonwoods but knew them at once.

Route 81 is mostly a dirt road instead of concrete as the map said but it is good. Man who owns the camp at Salina owns 160 acres of land with the city all around him, but they can't take over 20-acre tract into corporation without consent of owner. So he has all advantages without city tax, lights, water, etc. He owns a wheat farm in Canada and goes up to harvest every year. Drives on 81 clear there. Says it is a dirt road until it reaches North Dakota, then it is cement.

He picks and chooses travelers. Won't have any in his cabins that he doesn't like. First compliment of the season.

Went through Minneapolis, a pretty town, lots of shade trees and beautiful houses.

7 A.M. Heard our first MeadowLark. That's why the capitals.

7:15 A.M. Entering Cloud County.

8:15 A.M. Through Concordia, 6,000 inhabitants. Pretty city. Reached the land of "You bet you!"

One pretty house on top of a round hill rock cliff in front where road is cut out and stairs lead up to house.

9 A.M. Entering Republic County. Nice, straight long road through country. Very few cars, meadowlarks singing in the grass beside the road all day.

Saw first striped gopher, and a red-winged and a yellow-winged blackbird. Crops looking better. Camped at Osceola [Kansas]. Gas stove, electric light, garage attached. Shower bath in another building. All not very good. Looks to be clean but gives me the feeling it's not. Nero don't like the place much but we drove 168 miles today and this is the best we saw since 1 P.M. Cool morning, hot since noon with a following wind just about the speed we wanted to drive from 30 to 35, so poor Isabelle had a bad time again.

Stopped at 4 P.M.

Owner of cafe where we had dinner lived with his folks in Howell County, Missouri, when he was a boy. Said the ground was so rocky they had to dig out rock so they could scrape up soil to put around plant roots. I told him I didn't doubt it a bit, and that it was even worse in Douglas County, for there a man fell in his cornfield and broke his neck on the rocks.

EXPENSES	
Cabin & Garage	$1.25
Gas	1.63
Dinner	.80
Milk for Nero	.10
Oil for car	1.50
	$5.28

June 10

LEFT THE UGLY CAMP at 4:30 A.M. Nero tickled pink to get started. Drove through Columbus at 6 A.M. Beautiful German city. Rain last night. The air fresh and cool. No dust. Roads, these

Rose in Isabelle, the 1923 Buick that Laura and Almanzo drove to De Smet.

wonderful roads. Crossed Platte River flats and river on a long bridge, a short bridge, and another long bridge just before we entered Columbus. Each bridge a quarter of a mile long. One narrow and one wide enough to pass if each car drove on lenghthwise planks. Manly is spoiled by the wide smooth roads, so he could not stay on the planks. Says he don't believe he will be able to drive when he gets home.

Fine farming country, both sides of Columbus level and rich. Great, beautiful farm homes set in groves of large trees. Simply stunning, large houses, great hay and horse barns, hog houses, chicken houses, granaries. Each farm place looks like a small village. Big, round corncribs without the crib! Corn right outdoors all alone in the fields in those crib-shaped piles. Every building—even the pig creeps*—painted.

German Catholic country—Catholic churches now and then. Meadowlarks singing beside the road.

Stopped at Humphrey, 40 miles from last night's camp, for breakfast. Ate at a German bakery restaurant. Delicious coffee and Manly ate German cakes. I had the good German bread toasted with a great hunk of homemade butter, the best ever. Both breakfast and a pint of milk for Nero 35¢. A quaint little German place and town.

A field of peonies by the road. Peonies for sale. Saw a snow fence by the R.R.

Through Madison, a county seat, and headed for Yankton 90 miles north at 8:20 A.M. Passed a rabbit farm and a licensed fur farm all fenced, dog and cat tight. North from Madison about 20 miles 2 nice clean camps on a river, boats and fishing. Nicest kind of people, kind, cheerful, jolly.

---

*Separate areas for piglets to protect them from getting crushed.

Norfolk is a nice town, with a fine, clean, large camp, filling station, place to eat, etc. (like the one on the way to St. Louis), just north of town. Meridian Cottage Camp north of Norfolk on Highway 81. All farming done by horses, 4-horse teams. Often 8 horses working in a field. Very few cars on the roads even near the cities. Gosh, I'd forgotten there was such a farming country in the U.S. And my God it is a ruined country. Being sold out on taxes. Fifty of these wonderful farms now advertised for tax sale. Many already have been sold and the rest just hanging on. Will not be able to last much longer. Haven't made any profit on their farms for 10 years now.

The young man we were talking to at the filling station is very intelligent. He looked at our license plate and asked about conditions in Missouri. Said he saw people from everywhere and that was all they talked about—conditions—and they seemed to be the same everywhere.

The filling station man lost his 200-acre farm just recently, taxes and interest. His father has a 400-acre farm and his taxes amount to $100 a month.

Eastern loan companies are taking in the farms on their mortgages. People with federal loans are hanging on yet, but will not be able to make their payments unless there is a change in the prices of their produce. He said the places were not being kept up now. They were beginning to run down. Here is a home market for industry—steel, paint, R.R. and all if it could be used.

Pheasants—tame kinds but running wild—run across the road from one covert to the other.

Making hay all along the way. Alfalfa thick and high. Plowing corn, beautiful fields of corn, but late because of cold spring. Fields reaching from the road so far back that the great big horses look small. Eight and ten horses working on a field. Roads well marked. Every help given to keep one safe and the finest roads ever.

The man at the filling station said they were just beginning on cement in Nebraska and the taxes would be even higher. Well, I suppose there must be a good road for the farmers to walk out of the country on.

Eleven A.M. Getting into the breaks of the Missouri River, nearing Yankton.

Looking over the softly rolling country the colors are wonderful. The different shades of greens and yellows of the grasses, the soft, bright green of the new spring wheat. All shades of black and brown of the newly plowed soil with corn in straight green rows across it. Yellow alfalfa in bloom on each side of the road, a soft blue sky and clouds floating over all.

12 noon, Yankton, S.D.

Traffic was bad, Manly was tired and Nero and I nervous. Thought we would leave Nero in the car in a garage and eat, get postcards, etc. But trying to find a garage we drove through the traffic twice.

I thought if I could only get out of the traffic alive, I could die happily of fright and asked Manly to drive on and eat at the next town. We drove through the traffic again and at the next filling station were told that the next town was 70 miles away. Looks like the joke was on me.

We could only drive on, hoping that what he said was not true, eating some fruit we bought in Columbus.

Drove 20 miles and at the junction of highways 81 and 16 found some fairly decent cabins and stopped at 2 o'clock to spend the night. There is a short-order eating place here and a mile down 16 is a little town with more food, so we are all right. Tomorrow with good luck we should be at Grace's. We are only about 70 miles from there.

So here we are in South Dakota. Yankton certainly bids us hail and farewell.

You remember the farewell.

We don't like Kansas but are crazy about Nebraska. So far we don't like South Dakota. It is dry and trying to rain but can't. Drove 185 miles today.

EXPENSES

12 gal. gas	$1.97
Breakfast & Milk	.35
Cookies	.10
Cabin	1.25
Garage for car	.50
	$4.17

~~~

June 11

LEFT CAMP AT 5:30 A.M. Nice cool morning. Road finely graveled. Can see for miles in every direction. Crops look good in spite of freezing ice three nights last week. Our coats are none too warm this morning. There are lots of pheasants feeding by the roadside, running in the grass, picking bugs, and standing to look at us, gray ones and brown ones and dove colored and beautiful dark red ones like a bright leghorn cock in color with bright red on their heads.

A 160-acre cornfield. Meadowlarks singing. Nice farmhouse and awfully large farms. The country seems so quiet and peaceful. Houses on the road about 4 miles apart and no cars on the highway. We have driven two hours and met only one truck and two cars. None has passed us. At the side of the road far from any house was a group of signs, one following the other, spaced apart that read "For-the-land's-sake-eat-butter."

This country has the feeling we loved so much in the Ozarks when we first went there, but which it has lost, a feeling of quiet and peacefulness. But then the wind isn't blowing this morning.

Fine Durham cattle in pastures, cows, proving my contention that one doesn't have to sacrifice beef to produce milk.

Left highway 81, turning west on 34 to Howard, 8 miles. Had a wonderful breakfast in Howard. I had bacon and eggs and coffee, bread, and for the land's sake ate the best butter I've tasted in ages. Manly had bacon and eggs, pancakes and syrup and good old northern green tea. Nero had hamburger and a drink of water.

Took Highway 25 out at 9:10 A.M., headed for De Smet 26 miles north. Awfully dry wild prairie grass, dried up to the roots. Not a bit of moisture in the fields and the crops just standing. Girls herding some cows along the sides of the road

PHOTO COURTESY OF AUBREY SHERWOOD

An early photograph of Calumet Avenue, the main street in De Smet, in 1883.

because grass is so short and pastures are dead. It is greener in the road ditches.

Came to De Smet from the south, but the town is built out so far and roads are in different places so nothing looked natural. Went through a corner of town and on to Manchester.

Just out of Manchester met a rainstorm from the southwest. Clouds looked quite their old-fashioned way. The rain poured and we dodged into a garage until the shower was over, then drove around the corner to Grace's. She came out to meet us, surprised, for she had got my letter just yesterday. She is the same old Grace, only not looking very well. Arrived at 10:30 A.M.

EXPENSES

Gas	none
Breakfast	$ .90
Shave	.25
Fruit	.25
	$1.40

Manchester, June 12

GRACE SEEMS LIKE A STRANGER only now and then something familiar about her face. I suppose it is the same with me. Nate is nice but his asthma is very bad.

We all went to De Smet today. Manly and Nate went on their own and Grace and I went to Sassee's drugstore. Saw Mrs. Sassee and Merl. Mrs. Sassee is like herself only more so. Strong faced and dispositioned as of yore. She is running the store. Merl talked of Rose and their class in school. Went to Wilmarth's store. They didn't know me of course and I didn't care to know them. Sherwood was at Lake Preston.

HERBERT HOOVER LIBRARY

A photograph of Grace and her husband, Nate Dow.

Saw his sister whom I don't remember having known though she says I did. Ran around town awhile then sat at the music store waiting for Manly and Nate to show up. Stupid, tiresome, hot. I got tired of it and went by myself up the street. Grace was tired and her feet swollen so it was hard for her to walk. Just as I met Manly, a little, wrinkled old woman came across the street and spoke. It was Jennie Ross Wheat. The same in every way only older. Mr. Wheat is dead. Gaylord

Ross is in the north part of the state a helpless cripple. Jennie talked and talked as always. Finally we tore loose, found Nate and Grace and went to supper, dinner at a cafe. Very good, fine service, seemed a treat to Grace and Nate. Then home to a close, hot bedroom for the night.

~~~⁂~~~

June 13

MANLY AND I WENT TO DE SMET by ourselves in the afternoon. I went to the courthouse to examine records in Ma's estate. Found all in Carrie's name as we thought it should be. On the way to Green's law office saw Charley Dawley and Manly visiting on the sidewalk in the shade. Dawley seems unchanged.

Grace and I called on Mrs. Tinkham. She is a little bit of an old woman but seemed very natural. Called me Laura and kissed me and seemed very glad to see me. Harold is a man and more of a fool than ever. He horrified me. Chatted a bit and went on. Called on Green and heard the story of the estate practically as we knew of it. Then back to Manchester.

June 14

IN THE MORNING Manly took Grace and me to De Smet to the old house, where we looked over Ma's and Mary's things that had been stored in one room. Everything of value left there has disappeared. In the afternoon we all drove out to Nate's farm.

June 15

MANLY AND I WENT TO DE SMET in the afternoon. Called on Florence Garland Dawley. She is quite feeble, not at all well, and going the next day to Rochester [Minnesota] to Mayo's [clinic] with her son who is a doctor. Florence was sweet as could be and we talked of the old days of the hard winter when she taught the school before it was closed for lack of fuel and because it was too dangerous to go to the schoolhouse.

Called on Mrs. Green who is a very nice person and spoke so sweetly of Ma and Mary. Said Ma was a mother to her when she first came to De Smet and lived in the house with her. I like Mrs. Green.

Then Manly and I drove out past Pa's farm on the road from town across the slough, nearly in the place where Carrie and I walked to school and Manly used to drive Barnum and Skip as he came dashing out to take me on those long Sunday afternoon drives when I was seventeen.

The road is a highway now. The little sand hill south of where the old house used to be was all that looked natural. The highway turns east and runs along beside what used to be Bert Cornwell's tree claim. We went far enough to be opposite Boast's old farm but the crossroad was so bad we did not go over. Drove back to town and out past our old farms. The homestead has no buildings on it and is all a grain field over the hill. The school land between it and the tree claim is still grass. There were no buildings on the tree claim and only a few trees left. Al and Oll Sheldon's houses across the road still stand with additions. We drove on toward Spirit Lake. Country looks as it used to, but there are houses and barns where the prairie used to sweep unmarked. Crossroads so bad we did not go to the lake. Back to Manchester and another hot night. No water fit to drink. We all drank weak tea.

A view of the Ingalls homestead in De Smet, taken in 1947 by Garth Williams when he was doing research for his artwork for the Little House books.

June 16

MANLY WENT TO DE SMET and spent the morning loafing with Charley and Gay Barrows. In the afternoon I went with him and looked up some more of the records at the courthouse, and we called on Lillie Keating Armstrong and she took us to see Johnnie Armstrong, where he is janitor at the courthouse. She is the same flannel-mouthed Irishwoman as ever. Flattery! My gosh! Manly always falls for her and Johnnie hard. He enjoyed it and I was amused. It is funny how everyone who never would have been so familiar in the old days calls me Laurie and loves me so much, but in some way I like it. It all makes me miss those who are gone, Pa and Ma and Mary and the Boasts and Cap Garland.

June 17

MANLY NEARLY SICK TODAY and I'm not feeling so good. This awful wind blowing gets us both and Nero can't understand why he can hear and feel so much that he can't see. He growls at it now and then. After dinner we all went out to Nate's farm.

The crops are short and dry.

Went with Grace to vote in school election and then to a store where the Presbyterian Aid was holding a sale of food. The sale was a failure and they were having to take back what they had brought.

— ✲ —

June 18

GRACE AND NATE are both sick. Nate cannot lie down for the asthma but sits up in his chair all night.

Grace is on a diet for diabetes and her feet and hands are badly swollen with rheumatism. They made us very welcome but I helped with the work, etc. Nero likes Grace and Nate. Today the hot winds are blowing from the south. It is 98 in the shade and the dust is blowing in clouds along the roads and off the fields and even off the pastures. We can see only a little way through it. We are all suffering in spite of having the house shut to keep out the wind. Nero is frightfully affected, just as he is before an electrical storm at home. He pants and runs around and will not eat. Grace says, "He is so pitiful!"

We have done all the running around we care to do and are leaving tomorrow for Keystone.

Sorry to leave Grace but glad to start on again. "The sooner 'tis over the sooner to rest," in the rock house under the walnuts. Gosh! What a world. Russian lost in dust storm came to Nate's on the farm and when Grace opened the door he said "I'm loose! I'm loose" (lost). Manchester is an outlaw town. One man got his auto license, then everyone in town used it. Fifteen cars using the same license. If two wanted to go at the same time, one used one plate and the other the other one. The man came to Nate's and said, "I have my license plates now any time you want to drive your car come and get one." Families in town too poor to lay in a winter supply of coal so the town had a "Boston tea party," went boldly to the R.R. cars of coal and helped themselves. Laughing and calling to each other, they hauled it away, filled up the empty coal bins and stored a pile in an empty car.

The R.R. men couldn't prove ownership when they found the coal there so they had to leave it there even though no one knew who it belonged to or how it got there.

Bootleggers' headquarters is the pool hall—public rough and drinking but the best of good people, Grace says. Women weigh 200, 215, 247 and 300 lbs.

316

June 19

LEFT MANCHESTER 5:30 A.M. Real cool and cloudy, prairie is flat and monotonous and *dry*. Corn leaves are rolled from the drought. Potatoes are wilted. The country is all the same and to save me, I can't keep awake.

Toward noon it is awfully hot again and the wind is rising. Nero is sleeping soundly after his wretched night when it was so hot none of us could sleep. We had set up on the porch until 10 hoping it would be cooler then went to bed and lay sweat out while Nero panted. Now he is sleeping while I nod and start awake and sleep with eyes open trying to help Manly watch road signs and to be sure he stays awake while driving. Drove through Huron and on to Pierre. Had a good dinner at Blunt and good coffee. Country worse and worse. "Wide open spaces" indeed and believe me, they're dry!

Pierre is the capital of South Dakota but it has a population of only 2,500. Stopped at Midway Camp on the banks of the Missouri River just west of Pierre at 2 P.M. With good luck we'll be in Keystone tomorrow. I'm so sleepy I can hardly write.

Walked down to the Missouri River with Nero. It is a magnificent sweep of water 1,900 feet wide. There was a ferry there in 1817 where there is now the highway cement bridge. Monument to geographic center of North America, 9 miles east of Pierre. Lost my complexion somewhere between Manchester and Pierre.

EXPENSES

Gas 7 gal	$1.22
Dinner	1.00
Bread	.12
Cabin	1.00
	$3.34

Pierre, June 20

LEFT MIDWAY WITHOUT breakfast thinking we would eat at the first town we came to. We came to Ft. Pierre at 7:30 A.M. but everyone was sound asleep. We woke up the filling station man for gas but one look at the place decided us to let the hotel man sleep on. The next town was Philip, 92 miles from Midway Camp, and there we ate breakfast at 9 o'clock. Any time I don't feel like getting breakfast at home I shall have Manly drive us up to

Springfield. It is terribly dry all the way but cattle are fat running on the range, and small cactus are growing all over the pastures and by the roadside. It was so hot we stopped for an ice cream at a little filling station and I fed Nero an ice cream cone to cool him. He loved it. Had lunch at the New Underwood and got to Rapid City a little after noon. Went through a corner of the Badlands and took some pictures of Nero and me among the gutter mounds and fields. It was only 22 miles to Keystone, and after driving all over Rapid City to find Nate's cousin, only to learn she was not at home, decided to drive on and see Carrie that same day. There is no highway to Keystone and our directions were to drive 2 blocks south, 3 east, turn to the right and go straight ahead following the road that wound up around a hill. Up we went and up winding around the hill until Isabelle balked and backed and the brakes wouldn't hold her. I jumped out and blocked a wheel with a rock while Manly cussed because the brakes wouldn't hold the car "on a perfectly level road." It was so level that Isabelle would have backed to the bottom without the rock, and when we finally did reach the top she boiled and boiled, five times we stopped to let the engine stop boiling, but at last we arrived at Keystone.

Carrie during her working years in the early 1900s.

Carrie was on the walk before her house talking to her next-door neighbor. She had changed a great deal but I knew her. And of course she knew me when we stopped, for I had written her we were coming.

We got a cabin just across the street from her house beside a cold mountain brook and were very comfortably settled at 5 o'clock P.M.

Had supper with Carrie and met Dave and Harold,* who were about what we had expected them to be. Talked late then went to the cabin to bed.

Drove 166 miles.

EXPENSES

Gas 16 gal	$3.03
Breakfast	.50
Dinner	.50
Milk	.10
Bread & Doughnuts	.20
	$4.33

June 21

WE PLANNED AT BREAKFAST to go up Rushmore. I told Manly privately that I positively would not go a foot over the mountain roads with him driving. He simply cannot judge distance or grades in the Black Hills. The filthy smoke drifting in all the way from Pierre nearly to Rapid City is making a haze over all. Station man drove us and Carrie and

---

*Dave Swanzey was Carrie's husband and Harold was his son, Carrie's stepson.

The carving of Mount Rushmore as Laura may have seen it, starting with Washington's sculpture.

Nero up. The road up was good and it is only 8 miles.

At the studio everyone but the workmen are stopped. We could see the men working on Washington's face, held on by harnesses from above. A cloud of the granite dust was flying. The men wear masks for the protection but we were told they still breathe enough of the dust so they will not live long. The granite particles are so fine they settle and pack in the lungs.

We bought cards at the studio, looked our fill at the workings and went back to Keystone and supper.

Aubrey Sherwood* and wife were among the last sightseers allowed on the top of Rushmore. They went up all right but starting down she was afraid. "Oh, I'll fall!" she said. "I'll be killed!" Harold Swanzey was with them, and he had to carry her down on his back.

———

June 22

STARTED ON THE DRIVE to the Needles, Sylvan Lake, Game Lodge, etc. The man driving helped make the roads and had charge of Camp Galena for some time until politics put him out. Good dinner and lots of room for Carrie, Nero and me on the backseat.

The mountains grew steeper, the rocks greater as we drove on. The grades were steep and road narrow. Hill City first station, stopped for popcorn. Left Hill City on the Needles road, strange,

*Editor of *The De Smet News.*

tall, sharp pointed-rock particles. Stopped at the "Needle's Eye" and looked back into caverns and off into space over the hills, and valleys below. On again around cliffs on such sharp turns that it took careful driving and knowledge of the road to be safe.

Passed several places where cars have gone off. Mount Harney always in sight, its lookout station on the top looking like a rather small sock. There Forest Rangers watch the Hills for sign of fire, watch the weather and the game on the mountain. On some of the curves, large cars have to back and turn to get around. Came to Sylvan Lake in its hollow in the Hills. A beautiful sheet of water, clear and cold, deep to the edge. A summer resort hotel on the bank and a store for sale of postcards etc. near it.

Down a steep narrow path between two cliffs so high we couldn't see out. Over our heads were two great boulders that had lodged in the crack between the cliffs when the Black Hills were made. We came below the dam that made the lake. It was swung across a very narrow chasm between the cliffs. The water from the lake flowed over the top in a beautiful falls and went on its way, the Lord knows where.

Got a postcard from Sylvan Lake, then we went on to Camp Galena, headquarters for the National Guard and the Forest Rangers. Here were a large, comfortable community house, quarters for the guardsmen and rangers and a store made of the native rocks and woods. Necklaces of rose quartz and white crystallized quartz, rings and pins, paperweights, bookends, cigarette stands.

Got a pin of rose quartz for Rose, and one for Helen.* Manly got a paperweight for Rose and got more postcards. Had noon dinner, a fruit salad, mountain trout, mashed potatoes, new beets, lettuce and tomato salad, hot rolls with sweet butter and wild honey. For dessert Manly had pie, the rest of us ice cream. The coffee was simply delicious.

Carrie was horrified at the expense, but would you believe it was only .75 each! The service was good too. We took Nero the scraps and a drink of ice water and drove on to the Game Lodge, where the driver said, "Me and Coolidge used to sit and chat on the porch." The very porch where Coolidge decided he did "not choose to run." The lodge is of logs with rocks built up around the porch. There is a large rock fireplace at the end of

*Helen Boylston was a friend of Rose's.

the large room, with a portrait of Coolidge on one side of it and of Mrs. Coolidge on the other. There are easy seats, and curios and paintings all around the room. A smaller room off the end has a fireplace made of rose and crystal quartz, onyx, petrified wood and other beautiful rocks I don't know the name of. The whole thing was as lovely as a jewel. This small room was full of curios and souvenirs all for sale. Manly got Bruce* a tobacco pouch, but there was nothing prettier than what I had already got and we were a long way from home with space limited, both here and hereafter.

From the Game Lodge we went to the park where the animals are wolves, foxes, coyotes, badgers, possum, rabbits and even a poor eagle sitting on a perch. Didn't like it. The bears were comical and seemed very happy, with a pool to swim in or drink from and a deep cave in the cliff, where they hid until our driver fed one small bear some candied popcorn. The big bears heard him crunching it and came lumbering out of the cave, but the little bear hid behind some bushes and moved when the big ones came near, eating all the time as fast as he could and watching sharply. The big

*Bruce Prock helped Manly farm at Rocky Ridge.

bears were not hungry and waddled around, drank and scratched and took no notice of us outside their fence. There were five of them, black and brown and I'm glad there was a fence.

We drove down a side road for some ways to see the wild buffalo and the deer. Had a good view of buffalo—ugly, moth-eaten-looking creatures, lying and standing in the shade when we came near them and then they went farther away up a side hill, deeper into the wilds. The deer

[text is missing, entry continues on the same day] all the oufit teams wagons etc.

Great credit for building so good a stockade was given to two young Wisconsin lumbermen who had charge of the work. During the winter gold was discovered in and near the creek where it entered the surrounding hills. The party fought off the Indians and survived all the hardships, jubilant over their gold discovery. When they saw soldiers coming across the meadow in the spring, they threw wide the gates of the stockade to welcome them. The soldiers, under orders from President Grant, and his son Fred who was with them, took the members of the Gordon party prisoners, burned all their outfit and wagons just outside the stockade. The people were taken to Sioux City and turned adrift, without money or supplies. Immediately it was made known that a treaty had been signed with the Indians by which the Black Hills was opened to the whites. It was claimed that Fred Grant and his party were the first whites in and members of the Gordon party thought that was the reason for their eviction. But the Gordon Expedition is now given the honor. Someone else had their gold mine, but it is curious that no one who has marked it has ever had any luck, although it was a good prospect.

It gave me a queer feeling to walk along the creek and into the stockade, where Uncle Tom* had gone many, many times to peer through the peepholes at the corners along the sides of the log walks where he must so many times have watched to guard against Indian attack.

At the entrance to the little meadow stands the monument to the one woman of the party, Annie Tallent. The tablet with her name on the monument has been shot full of holes by tourists. It has been mended but is badly defaced. From here we went on to the old frontier town of Custer, with

---

*Laura's uncle Thomas Quiner, younger brother of her mother, Caroline, had gone prospecting with the Gordon party.

The stockade on French Creek where the Gordons spent a winter in 1874 looking for gold.

the widest streets ever. It is on the level ground of a valley. When the town was laid out, one man insisted that the streets should be wide enough for him to turn his team around in. It was of course four animals strung out and the man was somewhat drunk at the time, hence the amazing width of the streets.

329

It is a pretty town, clean and sweet. The beautiful rocks of the hills are built into the buildings. There is a park with a soldier monument built entirely of rocks, the black rock of the Hills, rose quartz, white crystal, mica, petrified wood, greens and yellows and blues in all sorts of mineral rocks, granite, the hardest in the U.S., and of different shades of gray and brown, and all sorts of combinations of one kind of rock growing with another, according to rules which a mineralogist would know. The rocks were laid in artistic combinations. It was a beautiful thing. In the park were large urns and vases and pedestals made of bits of clear rose quartz and white crystal and others. In a pavilion was an old stagecoach, a wreck and a relic, and there was a good-sized building full of museum pieces. One of them was a chunk of one of the original logs of the stockade, dug out of the ground when the restoration work was done. There were old guns and whips, knives and tommyhawks, specimens of all the ores and rocks of the hills and mounted specimens of all the birds and most of the animals native there, mountain lion, deer, wildcat, elk horns, deer antlers. There were pictures. Oh, it was a wonder place. We stayed and stayed and looked and looked until our driver got uneasy.

Then I got candy and ice cream for us all at a nice little place and we went on through the Hills or mountains, up and down, around and around until we came again to Hill City and from there on home over the road we started out on in the morning, to supper at Carrie's and bed in the cabin across the street and the creek.

The Black Hills are black hills, great black rocks standing above the pine tops in pinnacles and needles and cliffs. Small rocks are balanced on top of tall rocks with nowhere to have fallen from. Scottish bluebells grow on rocks with no sign of soil or even a crack to sustain them.

June 23

NEXT DAY CARRIE TOOK US to see a Mrs. Roy, who with her companion Mrs. Galliger lives out at the far end of the road beyond the camps. Eighty-five years old, straight as a pine, tall, with very bright blue eyes. Her house is at the base of a cliff and is covered with woodbine and is a marvel, with rose quartz and white crystal borders to her flower beds and walks, and an old oaken bucket in the backyard. All kinds of queer rocks and beautiful handiwork in her house, which is as clean as anything could possibly be. She is an old, old timer in the Hills and I am sure would tell many a story if one got to know her. She has read several of Rose's books and magazine stories and is eager for more, she likes them so much. We tore ourselves away at last because she was growing tired, and as she said, she had been down in Rapid City for a while and her heart hadn't got regulated since she came back. All morning Manly had talked with people at the filling station and Carrie and I visited.

June 24

NEXT DAY CARRIE AND I STAYED home with Nero while Manly and Dave visited some mines.

Then we packed up for an early start home next morning. Manly is awfully tired. Both our ears ring and our heads feel bad and Manly's aches terribly for two days now. Nero was nearly overcome with the heat for it is 105 in the middle of the day though *cold* at night. None of us seem to get used to the altitude and I think it best we hurry to lower levels.

The Black Hills are full of stories of Calamity Jane, how she took care of anyone who was sick

Carrie and her husband,
David Swanzey.

whether it was smallpox or diphtheria or whatever. How she drank and swore and played cards
and rode like a man. How she had many husbands
without formality of marriage or divorce, but only
one at a time. How she could be depended upon in
emergency and was a good sport always.

Once Calamity Jane and the pro tem husband
were riding out from the fort. Indians surprised
them and shot the man's horse. He told her to run

333

Martha Jane Canary earned her nickname, Calamity Jane, for her courage on the open prairie in the late 1800s.

for it, her horse was good and she could beat the Indians to the fort.

"What do you think I am?" she asked as she jumped from her horse, turned him loose, and dropped down beside the man behind the dead horse.

Her horse ran to the fort and the soldiers came out to see what had happened. They saw Calamity Jane and the man shooting at the Indians from behind the shelter of the dead horse. The Indians ran and the two were rescued.

Harold went fishing one day and brought back mountain trout, speckled trout, rainbow trout, Loch Leven trout, and for two days we almost lived on fish. The best I ever tasted.

———

June 25

LEFT KEYSTONE AT 4:30 A.M.

Carrie came down to the cabin to see us start. Car worked fine, mostly downgrade and going lower all the time. Our ears stopped roaring at Rapid City, where we had breakfast at the A.F. The waitresses were all mad about something and went around with their noses in the air. Miserable service so no tip and our waitress shortchanged herself

5 cents which was all to the good. The filling station young man was as nice as when we went up. It was heartening the way he wished us good luck.

Hot as blazes, frightful-looking hills. On 40 through the Badlands. Dinner at Kadoka good, on 16 East. Hot and a hot wind blowing. Country all dried up and brown. Car ahead and Manly said, "Well, anyway, we're not the only darn fools." Thought Nero would die of the heat. Pulled down the blinds to shade him, and the wind blew on him all the time but the wind was hot.

Highway 16 is "Custer Battlefield Highway." Runs all the way from Custer Battlefield in the Black Hills to Sioux Falls. Can follow it all the way from Keystone. 40 is just a detour to see the Badlands.

Tried to find place to stay from 3 o'clock on and stopped at Chamberlain on the Missouri River at 5 P.M. Cabins in the city park clean, nice, man on guard all night. Cabins airy, with windows and doors screened and fastened but not a curtain or blind of any kind. Gasoline stove and electric light. Electric light in yard so placed that it shone into every cabin and onto the head of the bed. I know now how a goldfish feels. A swimming pool in park filled from artesian well. Everybody swam.

I said, "The hot wind is blowing us out of Dakota again," and Manly said, "It's the last time it will ever have the chance."

Drove 266 miles.

EXPENSES

Gas	$2.28
Breakfast	.70
Dinner	.50
Ice cream	.10
Milk	.10
Cabin	1.00
	$4.68

June 26

OVERSLEPT, LEFT CAMP AT 6 A.M., but the first ones out. Crossed Missouri River on a bridge, narrow channel around ugly bare banks. City asleep as we drove through, up a hill and out into the open prairies. It has rained on this side of the river. Every slough and ditch is full of water. Big fields of corn, crops look fine. Working the land with horses. Open prairie, the first after the hill up from the river. Stopped and took Nero for a run, walked a long way down a side dirt road, just a track through the grass.

The dirt was black and soft underfoot, little hollows and small swells, meadow-larks singing—took me back a hundred years more or less. Saw a jackrabbit bound away and sit up like a stake. The first live jackrabbit I have seen. The highway has been plastered with dead ones all the way.

Had breakfast at White Lake 38 miles from camp. Nero very comfortable sleeping. Big cribs of old corn. Yesterday, even through that awful dry country, there were many big cribs of last year's corn.

Crossed Vermillion River. Dinner at Humboldt, 15 miles from Sioux Falls at 1:45 P.M., left Nero and the car in the shade and walked a block in the blazing sun. Wind is blowing hot now and we are almost directly south of De Smet and Manchester so I think hot winds are blowing there, on and on in the sun and the hot wind. This is hog country—all along the way we smell hogs till my stomach is fairly turned.

Crossed the line into Iowa at 4:30 P.M. Farewell Dakota and if forever still forever farewell. Stopped at some nice cabins in Rock Rapids at 5 o'clock. Cabin very clean and comfortable. I am waterlogged from drinking so much water since we stopped.

Have been taking the wrong road often for two

days, sometimes 2 miles beyond an intersection before there is a highway marker, always some distance.

Drove 183 miles.

EXPENSES

Gas	$2.94
Breakfast	.86
Dinner	.60
Sardines & Peaches	.50
Cabin	1.25
	$6.15

~~~

June 27

TEA, BREAD & BUTTER, doughnuts in cabin. Drove away at 5:10 A.M. Nice cool morning, Nero very comfortable. Beautiful rolling country still smelling of hogs. Nice groves around the buildings. So on into Sioux County, Iowa.

Came to a little town not on the map and missed the name. A large sign said, "Friendly Warning. Go Slow! Streets patrolled." Another sign at town's edge said, "End of state maintenance."

Filling station man told us land was worth

from $100 to $225 an acre. The same land sold during the boom for $750 an acre. Everyone is broke, farms mortgaged for more than they are worth. Roads are well marked and good. Such a relief after being lost so much for 2 days.

Onto pavement, through Le Mars at 7 A.M., Sioux City at 8 A.M. on 75 all the way from Rock Rapids to Council Bluffs. Cornfield continuous for miles and miles, men plowing corn all cooling their teams. Hotter than blazes. Kept stopping to cool Nero. Stopped at 4:30 P.M. because we found fine cabins at Hamburg, on a detour for road working. Nice place to stay. Filling station people asked us to sit in their yard and to be in the shade. Cabins new and clean, fresh painted and airy, but it was sweltering hot all night. The sweat ran down my face as I lay facing and right against a window.

Drove 127 miles.

EXPENSES

Gas 15 gal	$2.40
Dinner	.75
Packing pump	.25
Cabins	1.25
	$4.65

June 28

LEFT CAMP AT 5:30 A.M. Still on detour to Maryville by way of Phelps City and Rock Port. Across country, no signs, asking the way at farmhouses. Uphill and down, hill after hill. Breakfast at Rock Port while Nero sat in garage. Eighteen hills! Stopped to cool Nero and the engine. Hot and following wind at Burlington Junction. Had fan tightened and wheels oiled. Nero cooled on cement floor. Two miles west left 18 and took 41 to St. Joseph, cement highway. Detoured at Cameron about 4 miles then back on cement. Nero was so hot we got ice cream for Nero and Manly and pop for me.

Then on 69 to Excelsior Springs. Beautiful place, what I could see of it, watching signs through the traffic. Lake full of people in bathing suits or less. Richmond a nice town, but no cabins. Crossed the Missouri River on a great bridge at Lexington. Wonderful view of the river both ways. No cabins. Harriett a pretty, small town. Tourist rooms full. Cabins on lake only 2 miles out we were told over a good dirt road, so we drove about 3 miles over an awful road and learned we were headed for a regular lake resort a mile farther on. Took an angling road back to the highway. Oh well, it was a day of detours. Higginsville a nice place but no cabins. Must go on to junction of 18 with 40 and there were cabins all along the way. Late and at least 20 miles farther to go. Stopped at Oliver's Station at 7:30 P.M. Good cabins, meals. Cooled Nero with an electric fan while we found a scrap of shade at a house in town by a filling station. Took Nero out in it, gave him cold water to drink and poured cold water over him. Let him lie on the grass in the shade while we had an ice cream soda, then on again, twice more we had to stop and cool him. He seems to be all right but is still panting. There is absolutely no place that is cool and no shade on the road. Inside a building is hotter than Hades and Nero can't stand it. What a world!

Extra good wheat being harvested all along the way. Nice-looking country, good cattle and horses, but the country smells of sweet clover and timothy hay instead of hogs.

Ate.

Drove 233 miles.

EXPENSES

Gas	$2.00
New spark plugs etc.	4.00
Oiling wheels & Tightening fan	.26
Breakfast	.40
Ice cream & Pop	.20
Pop	.05
	$6.91

June 29

LEFT CAMP AT 6:10 A.M. Manly not feeling good, effects of long drive over bad roads yesterday.

Hope there are no detours today. Awfully warm morning. Good wheat along the way. 6:40 A.M. on 65 headed for Springfield, Nero sleeping peacefully. The wind cool and not strong. Through Sedalia, Warsaw, Buffalo. Country from near Sedalia on, dryer and hotter.

Stopped at Fair Grove to get the car washed and have a bite to eat. Breakfast unsatisfactory, coffee and all not good, the water at Fair Grove is so low they cannot wash cars. They are about to be out of any water.

Later, took Nero with us to a cafe and had a good plate lunch, sweet corn, beans, potatoes, roast pork and gravy, good coffee and ice cream.

Fed Nero scraps and gave him a drink. Then on to Springfield and go for home. Stopped at Rogersville for gas and phoned Rose. Lost track of gas and other expenses, accounting no good all the way, but cost of trip $120 for 4 weeks and 2,530 miles.

LAURA INGALLS WILDER was born in 1867 in the log cabin described in *Little House in the Big Woods*. As her classic Little House books tell us, she and her family traveled by covered wagon across the Midwest. She and her husband, Almanzo Wilder, made their own covered-wagon trip with their daughter, Rose, to Mansfield, Missouri. There Laura wrote her story in the Little House books, and lived until she was ninety years old. For millions of readers, however, she lives forever as the little pioneer girl in the beloved Little House books.

ROSE WILDER LANE was born in 1886 to Almanzo and Laura Ingalls Wilder. Like her mother, she was a prolific writer, and the author of works of both fiction and nonfiction, including the bestselling *Let the Hurricane Roar*. She died in 1968.

The late **ROGER LEA MacBRIDE** was born in New York State and was a graduate of Harvard Law School. He was a friend of Rose Wilder Lane's and the author of the Rose Years novels.

A
LITTLE HOUSE
TRAVELER

Laura Ingalls Wilder was born in the Big Woods of Wisconsin on February 7, 1867, to Charles Ingalls and his wife, Caroline.

When Laura was still a baby, Pa and Ma decided to move to a farm near Keytesville, Missouri, and the family lived there about a year. Then they moved to land on the prairie south of Independence, Kansas. Laura based her third book, *Little House on the Prairie*, on the years she and her family lived there. After two years in their little house on the prairie, the Ingallses discovered that the land they lived on belonged to the Osage Indians, so they went back to the Big Woods to live in the same house they had left three years earlier! This time the family remained in the Big Woods for three years.

In the winter of 1874, when Laura was seven, Ma and Pa decided to move west to Minnesota. They found a beautiful farm near Walnut Grove, on the banks of Plum Creek.

The next two years were hard ones for the Ingallses.

Swarms of grasshoppers devoured all the crops in the area, and Ma and Pa could not pay off all their debts. The family decided they could no longer keep the farm on Plum Creek, so they moved to Burr Oak, Iowa.

After a year in Iowa, the family returned to Walnut Grove again, and Pa built a house in town and started a butcher shop. Laura was ten years old by then, and she helped earn money for the family by working in the dining room of the hotel in Walnut Grove, babysitting, and running errands.

The family moved only once more, to the little town of De Smet in Dakota Territory. Laura was now twelve and had lived in at least twelve little houses. Laura grew into a young woman in De Smet, and met her husband, Almanzo Wilder, there.

Laura and Almanzo were married in 1885, and their daughter, Rose, was born in December 1886. By the spring of 1890, Laura and Almanzo had endured too many hardships to continue farming in South Dakota. Their house had burned down in 1889, and their second child, a boy, had died before he was a month old.

First, Laura, Almanzo, and Rose went east to Spring Valley, Minnesota, to live with Almanzo's family. About a year later they moved south to Florida. But Laura did not like Florida, and the family returned to De Smet.

In 1894, Laura, Almanzo, and Rose left De Smet for good and settled in Mansfield, Missouri.

When Laura was in her fifties, she began to write down her memories of her childhood, and in 1932, when Laura was 65 years old, *Little House in the Big Woods* was published. It was an immediate success, and Laura was asked to write more books about her life on the frontier.

Laura died on February 10, 1957, three days after her ninetieth birthday, but interest in the Little House books continued to grow. Since their first publication so many years ago, the Little House books have been read by millions of readers all over the world.

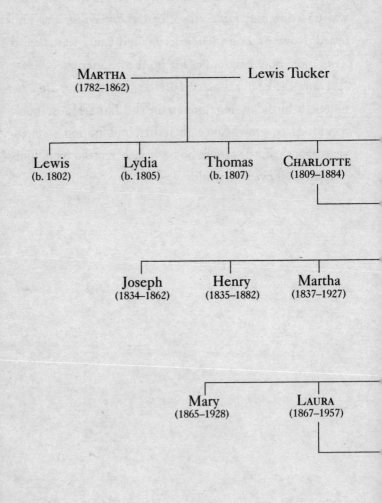

MARTHA (1782–1862) ——— Lewis Tucker

Lewis (b. 1802) Lydia (b. 1805) Thomas (b. 1807) CHARLOTTE (1809–1884)

Joseph (1834–1862) Henry (1835–1882) Martha (1837–1927)

Mary (1865–1928) LAURA (1867–1957)

The Little House
⦇ Family Tree ⦈

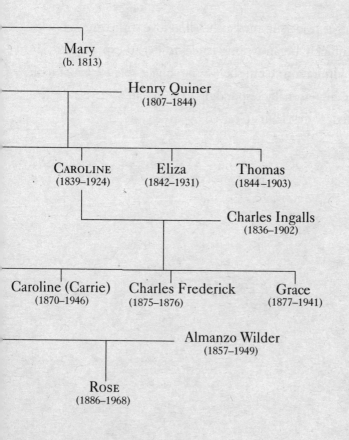

Mary
(b. 1813)

Henry Quiner
(1807–1844)

CAROLINE
(1839–1924)

Eliza
(1842–1931)

Thomas
(1844–1903)

Charles Ingalls
(1836–1902)

Caroline (Carrie)
(1870–1946)

Charles Frederick
(1875–1876)

Grace
(1877–1941)

Almanzo Wilder
(1857–1949)

ROSE
(1886–1968)

⚜ LETTERS TO LAURA ⚜

Younger readers immediately fell in love with Laura's books, and quickly began writing letters to her to express their joy and admiration. Until she was no longer able to, Laura took pride in personally responding to each letter. Here are a few fan letters that Laura received over the years.

Minneapolis Minn.
June 3, 1937

Dear Mrs. Wilder,
Our teacher read the two
books that you wrote.
I love them.
I want to know if Jack hurt
himself and do you wish
you were a little girl again
with your Ma and Pa. I hope
you like our posters and I
wish you a happy vacation.
Your friend Lee Thomas

I am 6 and ½
I am in the First
grade. I cut out your
picture from the
paper Love
Elizabeth Mary Plotz

Jan. 27, 1944

Dear Mrs. Wilder

I have read all your your books except On The Banks Of Plum Creek which doesn't seem to be in the 42nd Street Library. I was very ~~happy~~ excited when I read the book Hard Winter. I wondered how you lived through all those blizzards. How come the winds didn't blow your house away? How did you feel when you had to be a school teacher because ~~was~~ Mary was blind? I feel very sorry for her. My little twin sisters want to know if Grace, Carrie and Mary are still living. Do you still want to get even with you teacher Eliza Jane Wilder because she did those mean things to Carrie? I wish you could write some books about the life of Carrie and Grace later on. I think Grace was cute when she asked Pa if his nose is ~~for~~ frozen. Weren't you afraid when you ~~slide~~ slid on Silver Lake and saw the Big Buffalo Wolf? IF I was in your place then I would be so scared that I'd run away without Carrie. You were real brave to wait for Carrie. I wish I lived with you all through your life.
        Yours Truly
        Emily Mazur

10

Kaiulani School

783 North King St.

Dear Mrs Wilder,   May 5, 1948

I have read many of your books, which
I borrowed from the library of our school
Now I'm reading one of your books call "The
Long Winter." I have already finished reading
"Little House in The Big Woods" "Little House
on the Praire" "On the Banks of Plum creek"
and "By The Shores of Silver Lake." All of the
books were very interesting I have enjoyed them
very much. Many other children are also enjoying
reading your books.

I am a Chinese boy I came from
China about two years ago. Now I am in
the fifth grade and working hard. I have
just started to enjoy reading books. I like
your books the best because they are so
interesting and exciting. I hope someday
you will come to Hawaii and write a
story about us.

Mahalo

Johnson Yee

11

LAURA'S FINAL LETTER TO ROSE

Laura continued to write to Rose regularly throughout her life, and three days before Laura died, she composed a heartfelt letter to her daughter.

July, 30th 1952

Rose Dearest,

When you read this I will be gone and you will have inherited all I have.

Please give to the Laura Ingalls Wilder Library in Mansfield all that is left in my private library after you have taken from it want you want for yourself. This includes the framed testimonials from Chicago, California and the Pacific North West.

My jewelry is unique and should not be carelessly scattered. Do with it as you wish but preserve it in someway if you can.

We were proud of my Havaland china but loved best the English made blue Willow ware. Do as you please with all the china, but I wish you might use it.

The persimon-wood chair and the cypress stand-table that Manly made belong to Silas Seal.

My love will be with you always
                                    Mama Bess
                        (Laura Ingalls Wilder)

COME HOME
∽ TO ∾
LITTLE HOUSE